MW00960657

Writing as Anne Frasier

Hush, *USA Today* bestseller, RITA finalist,
Daphne du Maurier finalist (2002)
Sleep Tight, *USA Today* bestseller (2003)
Play Dead, *USA Today* bestseller (2004)
Before I Wake (2005)
Pale Immortal (2006)
Garden of Darkness, RITA finalist (2007)
Once Upon a Crime anthology, Santa's Little
Helper (2009)
The Lineup, Poems on Crime, Home (2010)
Discount Noir anthology, Crack House (2010)
Deadly Treats Halloween anthology, editor and
contributor, The Replacement (September 2011)
Once Upon a Crime anthology, Red Cadillac (April
2012)
Woman in a Black Veil (July 2012)
Dark: Volume 1 (short stories, July 2012)
Dark: Volume 2 (short stories, July 2012)
Black Tupelo (short-story collection
Girls from the North Country (short story, August
2012)
Made of Stars (short story, August 2012)
Stars (short story collection, August 2012)
From the Indie Side (February 2014)
Stay Dead (2014)

Writing as Theresa Weir

The Forever Man (1988)

Amazon Lily, RITA finalist, Best New Adventure
Writer award, *Romantic Times* (1988)

Loving Jenny (1989)

Pictures of Emily (1990)

Iguana Bay (1990)

Forever (1991)

Last Summer (1992)

One Fine Day (1994)

Long Night Moon, Reviewer's Choice Award,
Romantic Times (1995)

American Dreamer (1997)

Some Kind of Magic (1998)

Cool Shade RITA winner, romantic suspense
(1998)

Bad Karma, Daphne du Maurier award,
paranormal (1999)

Max Under the Stars, short story (2010)

The Orchard, a memoir (September 2011)

The Man Who Left , a memoir and *New York Times*
bestseller (April 2012)

The Girl with the Cat Tattoo (June 2012)

Come As You Are (October 2013)

The Geek with the Cat Tattoo (2013)

He's Come Undone (2014)

THE MAN WHO LEFT

Theresa Weir

BP

Belfry Press

Saint Paul, Minnesota

Prologue

Miami Beach, Florida, late fifties

He answered the knock to see a woman and two young kids standing on the front step of his Miami Beach rental house, the woman clutching her purse straps nervously with both hands. It was easy to see they'd arrived from a cold climate; they looked out of place in their winter clothes and pale winter skin. It took him a moment to realize these people were his wife and kids. As soon as he recognized them, he wanted to slam the door and lock it, go back to five minutes ago, before the knock, when he'd just finished his shower and was looking forward to heading out for breakfast with the guys.

"We got tired of waiting, so we thought we'd surprise you," Nan said.

Surprise wasn't what he'd call it, especially since he'd never expected to see any of them again. Stunned. Dismayed. Those were better words. He'd been gone four months, but they already seemed like strangers, and most days they no longer existed for him. In another few months he would have forgotten them completely.

Warren had been one of many young men who'd pursued Nan when she was single. He liked to win, and she'd been the biggest prize in town. But now … He'd packed up and left, hoping she'd forget about him as quickly as he'd forgotten about her. But here she was.

The kids. If she hadn't brought the kids, then maybe it wouldn't have been so bad.

He finished buttoning the shirt he'd slipped on before she'd knocked and turned his day upside down. It wasn't the kind of shirt anybody wore back in Iowa. It was a coral color, with a matching set of creases that ran down both sides, and a straight hem he didn't tuck in. A shirt a hip guy might wear, a cool cat.

He hadn't felt bad about leaving them. She'd betrayed him. She'd promised him things, not in words, but in actions, behavior. She'd promised him a rich and exciting life, but she hadn't delivered. A lie. It had all been a lie, and if anybody had been wronged it was him. Women tricked men. That's what they did.

Standing on the sidewalk, the girl clung to her mother's brown skirt, peeking out at him with big eyes, a shy smile hovering around her mouth. The boy was strolling around the yard, hands on his hips, examining plants and dirt and the sky like some little professor.

He'd come so close to forgetting them.

Warren had made friends here. Drinking buddies. Work buddies. Good guys. He hadn't told any of them he was married. He hadn't thought about the possibility of her following him. He figured that after some time passed he'd send a letter letting her know it was over, so there'd be no need to tell the new people in his life about her or the kids.

"What are you doing here?" he asked.

"I wrote, but you didn't answer. I would have called," she said. "But you never got a phone."

He had a phone; he'd just kept that information from her. He hadn't wanted her to call.

"How long are you staying?" He had no desire to invite her inside. He vaguely imagined her and the kids going to some dive of a motel, staying a few days, maybe swimming in the pool with their white skin, then piling back in the car to return to Iowa. The kids were now making noise the way they always did. The girl was screaming and crying, and she had red fingerprints on her arm. The boy was laughing.

Warren felt a moment of outrage toward the boy whose favorite pastime was tormenting his sister, but the outrage quickly shifted toward the woman who was trying to ruin his life again.

His wife's father had been one of the most brilliant men Warren had ever known. He was an inventor who'd designed and built an engine that could get eighty miles to a gallon, but lost efficiency at a high speed. It had just been a matter of time until the old man figured it out. Except he'd died unexpectedly. Just dropped dead from a heart attack at age fifty, and his inventions died with him. The whole family fell apart after that, and Nan had become a lot less interesting.

"Staying?" Nan asked with a baffled expression. "I sold the house in Iowa and we're moving here. Our furniture is on the way."

No.

"Go say hi to Daddy." His wife pushed the girl toward him. Sometimes Warren suspected Nan of using her pregnancies to keep him from leaving. Later, she used the kids themselves.

The girl came and stood in front of him, nervous and shyly waiting for some reaction. Unable to ignore her any longer, Warren lifted his daughter into his arms.

The past four months vanished. He felt the compactness of her body, smelled the sweetness of her skin and the sweat and shampoo of her hair. He remembered putting her to bed and kissing her goodnight.

She smiled at him and patted a chubby palm against his cheek, almost as if to comfort him. "Daddy."

He pressed his lips to her soft cheek, and he felt the blossom of something in his chest that he didn't want to feel.

"So you had a long car ride, huh?" he asked, pulling back to look at her face.

"We saw the ocean and palm trees." She couldn't pronounce her Rs very well, and she said twees rather than trees.

Now the boy was there looking up at him. He was too big to be held, so Warren put the girl down, then squatted in front of the other child. "Have you been taking care of things?" he asked. "The man of the house? Or have you been picking on your sister?"

The boy made an important face. People were drawn to his dark curly hair, and the way he talked like a well-educated man even though he was a little kid. "I've been taking care of things," he said.

They didn't embrace, but Warren ruffled the kid's curly hair, then straightened. "I've got to get to work." He looked across the yard as if searching for a visual escape. A car was parked by the mailbox. Someone was in it. Oh, God. Nan's brother.

Warren hated to admit it, but he was afraid of Nan's brothers, afraid of what they might do if they found out he'd dumped her, which was another reason he'd moved to Florida. He didn't want any of them beating the crap out of him again. And they were an odd bunch. So brooding and intense and alive in a way he didn't understand, in a way that was alien to him, a way that made him uncomfortable. If you asked him, they were all too smart for their own good, talking about art and books and movies and music, things Warren didn't care about and didn't understand. But there was Sammy sitting in the car. And was that Nan's mother in the backseat? Yes. Nan hadn't left her family in Iowa; she'd brought the clan with her. And she would expect him to support her kids, her mother, and her brother. He felt himself getting sucked under, pulled under. He couldn't deal with this now.

"I have to go to work." He started walking toward his car, a big blue Pontiac convertible parked in the driveway. He looked like one cool cat behind that steering wheel. But he wouldn't look so cool with a wife and kids.

Nan followed at his heels. "Maybe we can come down later this afternoon," she said. "Maybe you can show us your boat. I'd like to see it."

"The marina isn't a place for kids."

"I'll leave them here."

He didn't want any of them around. He didn't want any of them down there. "Not today," he said. "I'm too busy today." He hadn't even touched her.

She gave him a tremulous smile. "Maybe tomorrow then."

"Yeah, maybe tomorrow." He would figure something out. Figure out how to keep her away from his new life.

"What time will you be home for dinner?" she asked.

"Don't wait for me." He didn't want to encourage her or give her any ideas. He didn't want her to think they were going to be a family.

*

A woman in a white Mercedes pulled up at the end of the dock and got out of her car. To Warren she looked like someone from a movie, with her blond, swept-back hair and bright orange lipstick, her big gold necklace and big gold rings, giant black sunglasses, and a pale blue scarf wrapped around her neck.

He knew who she was. Everybody knew who she was. Eve Briggs, one of the richest divorcees in the area. And just to have something to do so life didn't get too boring, she owned a small fleet of deep-sea fishing boats that catered to the elite and wealthy of Miami Beach.

Right now she was watching three men as they tried to dock one of her boats. This was their third try at getting it in the slip, and the third failure. She blew out a disgusted breath and strode angrily down the dock, right past Warren, so close that he smelled her perfume and her hairspray and her nail polish. And a promise that was different from the promise his wife had made him years ago.

The boat was wedged at an angle, one corner near enough to the dock that she was able to jump on board. Once there, she elbowed the captain out of the way, reversed the craft and gunned the engine, water churning. Within two minutes, as Warren watched with open admiration, the boat was docked neatly in the slip. He couldn't hear the conversation on board, but it was obvious she was chewing out the captain. Moments later she was back on the dock, smoothing her hair with one hand, adjusting her white top. With something that seemed like a second thought, she paused on the way to her car and stared at Warren through her dark sunglasses. "Can you dock a boat?" she asked. Even her accent sounded rich, a combination of upper East Coast and British royalty. And why not? Her ex-husband was the prime minister of the Bahamas. She ran in circles Warren could only dream of.

Up close, she looked a lot older than she did from a distance. He'd heard she'd had a facelift, but you could have fooled him because her mouth was surrounded by a network of lipstick-filled lines. He didn't think she could ever have been pretty, but pretty didn't make any difference. She was powerful, and that elevated her to a level that had nothing to do with beauty. He'd never known a powerful woman, and he wondered what it would be like to sleep with her. She had at least twenty years on him, but he was still intrigued with the idea of sharing her bed.

He could smell gasoline and creosote and dead fish and damp shipyard rope and salt water and barnacles, and he could hear the sound of water lapping against pilings, along with the slow knock of boat hulls. As the Florida sun beat down, he sensed his destiny in that moment as he stood in front of the woman.

He could see himself reflected in the lenses of her sunglasses, and beyond himself, he could just make out the shape of her eyes.

"I can't dock a boat like you just did," he said, trying his best to come across as polite without appearing overly interested. He knew how to work women. It was one of his biggest strengths. "But I can dock—" he paused for effect "—a boat." He blinked and looked at her with complete innocence on the remote chance she was playing it straight.

"I'm looking for a new captain, and I've seen you around. But you look awfully young. How old are you?"

"Thirty." He added a couple of years to his age, and he thought the nice round number sounded good. She was at least fifty. His mother was fifty.

"Think you can handle the job?"

He had his own boat, but it was falling apart, and he'd been struggling to scrape up the money for repairs while doing a lot of the work himself. It was coming along, but now, with his wife and kids showing up …

Looking at the divorcee, he no longer had any interest in his boat. His boat bored him. "I can handle it."

"You have to work long hours. And since I'm single, I sometimes need someone to escort me to social functions. In fact, I have one coming up next week. Will that be a problem?"

"Not at all."

"Are you unattached?"

The marina workers and the deckhands gossiped like a bunch of old woman, and he'd heard the gossip about Eve. About how, ever since her divorce, she'd hopped from one young man to the next, leaving a trail of broken marriages behind her. The deckhands called the men her pets.

Was he unattached? Yesterday he would have said yes, but Nan might show up at the marina, and he didn't want to get caught in a lie. "I'm married, but I don't plan on staying that way." He liked that answer. He decided it made him seem more interesting, and it let her know that he was willing to change his whole life for her. And he was.

She smiled, then tipped back her head and laughed in delight. She reached out and stroked his shoulder, and he was glad he'd worn the coral shirt. "Join me for a cocktail at six o'clock in the marina lounge. A business drink."

He nodded. He had a cruise scheduled for late afternoon, and his wife was expecting him home for dinner. He smiled back, and even though Eve had removed her hand from his arm, he could still feel her long nails with their red, shiny polish. He wanted her to touch him again. With her next to him, he could quit struggling to stay afloat, quit fighting for every dime he made. He sensed that she could take care of him. Like a mother took care of a child, and like someone took care of a pet. And he had no problem being someone's pet. He wanted to be her pet. Maybe her last pet.

One of the worst days of his life had suddenly turned into one of the best. He smiled back at her. "I'll be there."

Chapter 1

Florida, present day

They arrive in a car and leave in a coffin. That's the big joke about Florida, but it's true. People flock here in the twilight of their lives, abandoning support of family and friends, traveling two thousand miles from their own history and their own past and anything connected to who they once were. By the time they realize their mistake, by the time they realize that now they are little more than this cane, this walker, this wheelchair taking them from doctor to doctor, it's too late. They're too unhealthy and poor to move back. And anyway, the old house is gone, sold for less than it was worth in order to get to this new land as quickly as possible because the clock is ticking. Many, like my father, end up too feeble and weak to return to their old homes for as much as a drive-by, something he talks of doing. Maybe just a glimpse would remind him of who he once was instead of an old man with no identity other than the geezer with a bad memory who shows up at the same bar every night at exactly six o'clock and waits for the bartender to automatically give him a glass of red wine and a sandwich.

"This is the best place I've ever lived," my father says as he struggles to get out of my rental car. His dead wife's words, parroted by him in the hopes that if repeated enough he will begin to believe them.

This isn't the Florida of Disneyworld. This is a bleak Florida that feels isolated and forgotten, a place painted in depression and disinterest. Rotten buildings originally bright pastels, chipped, faded, crumbling, growing out of weedy lots and speaking loudly of days that are no longer here and will never return. This is the land of hanging chads and oil spills, of things gone horribly wrong. My father, with white hair that used to be black, and sharp bones that poke from beneath his plaid shirt and beige slacks, looks a part of this Florida, the heat rounding his shoulders and pressing him nearer the ground as he drags his feet through the sand to the fruit stand located on a two-lane highway—a corner staked out under the shadow of a mega church. God must live in Florida.

"Why did we come here?" my dad asks.

For a moment I wonder if he's talking about Florida in general, but I quickly realize he means the fruit stand.

His life has been a series of mistakes and denials of those mistakes, so he's not going to start admitting to them now at the age of seventy-six.

"Apples," I tell him. "I'm going to bake an apple pie."

"Oh." He's uninterested.

"Do you like apple pie?"

"Sure, I do." But he doesn't seem certain. He seems puzzled that I would be on a quest for apples.

Under the tent that gives us respite from the glaring sun, I spot two varieties: Red Delicious and Granny Smith. "We want Granny Smith," I tell him, just to keep the conversation going. He's not looking at any of the produce, and the air of perplexed boredom continues to hover around him. He doesn't care about Red Delicious or Granny Smith. I pick out a few apples and put them on the counter. "Do you like honey?" I ask. I lift a small bottle of Tupelo honey.

"I think so." He's not impressed to hear how hard Tupelo honey is to harvest, and how rare. Such things have never mattered to him.

I add the honey to my purchase.

Dad digs out his wallet and begins to thumb through bills with renewed focus.

"I'm getting it," I tell him.

"No you're not." He can't remember that he's sixty thousand dollars in debt and living on social security. I finally convince him to put away his wallet; I pay, and we head back to the rental car I picked up last night at the Gainesville airport.

His house is located in a confusion of homes built in the sixties. Mostly ranch style on a mixture of curved and straight roads, a subdivision in what had once been a suburb, but now feels a part of the city of Ocala. A land of no sidewalks. I don't know why that disturbs me so much, but it does. When I'm in a city I want a grid and sidewalks. I want it to make sense.

Nobody knows why my father and Eve moved here from Oklahoma, a place they'd lived for forty years. I was told they were moving to a retirement community near Orlando. This is not a retirement community, but rather a neighborhood for young families, and my dad's home is located ninety miles from Orlando.

The house itself is a cheap imitation of the house they left in Oklahoma, as if they'd deliberately tried to make it seem like the same place. But upon closer inspection, the shoddy construction is obvious. The need to duplicate makes their move all the more confusing.

His wife has been gone a year, dead at age ninety-seven.

Once inside, we feed the dogs, two Dalmatians. One of Eve's expensive hobbies had been raising show dogs, most of which stayed in kennels where someone else cared for them. At one time she had no idea how many dogs she had, but these are the only two left. They've never been trained, don't recognize commands, but still manage to be charming in their ignorance.

The house is a shrine to the dead spouse. The walls are covered with her dog-show ribbons, fishing trophies, and photos spanning almost a hundred years. Before meeting my dad, Eve was married to the prime minister of the Bahamas, and there are even framed pictures of her with a young Queen Elizabeth.

My mother never suspected an affair.

"You'd better watch out," a friend had warned. "It won't be the first marriage she's broken up."

My mother had laughed at the ridiculousness of it. "She's old," she'd said. "Old enough to be his mother."

It was true. And even more awkward, people often mistook Eve for my dad's grandmother when they were out in public.

"And she's fat. And ugly. And boring. There's nothing going on."

But there was. I was too young to analyze my feelings, but later I came to understand that when a man betrays his wife, he also betrays his children.

My dad was working for Eve, piloting one of her deep-sea fishing boats, when she asked if he would escort her to a public function, if he would be her date for the night. "It would be lovely if I could walk in with a handsome young man on my arm," she'd told him. When she found out he didn't own a suit, she gave him money for a tuxedo.

My mother helped him find an outfit and helped him dress for the occasion.

"Why aren't you going?" I asked my mother.

"I wasn't invited. And even if I had been, I don't think I'd go. It's some formal, dull event." She'd turned to my father, adjusting his tie. "Remember your grammar. Don't say *ain't*. Eve wouldn't like that. Don't say *I seen*. It's *I saw*. No crude jokes and no cussing."

I thought he looked quite handsome, if only he hadn't been sweating so much. Like a boy playing dress-up. I wished I could go.

That night he didn't come home, and the next day he returned in wrinkled clothes, smelling of cigarettes and perfume, but buzzing with excitement. "The party lasted until three in the morning, so she said I could stay at her house," he told us.

"Where did you sleep?" my mother asked.

"In a guestroom. And in the morning, the table was set by maids in pink uniforms with white caps and aprons, and a chef stood behind us with his hands folded and waited to be told what we'd like for breakfast. There was more than one course, with silverware I didn't know what to do with." He shook his head in amazement.

"Maybe she'll adopt you," my mother said.

They both laughed.

"There's another engagement coming up next week, and she'd like me to go."

"Is she paying you? Surely she can't expect you to escort her to these things on your time off, take you away from your family without paying you something."

"She hasn't mentioned money, and I didn't want to ask."

"Christmas is coming. Maybe there'll be a bonus for you."

He plopped down on the couch and lit a cigarette, his eyes far away. "It was like going somewhere with the queen. You can't believe the way she lives and the people she knows. It's another world."

But now the queen was dead.

Nothing on the walls say this is my father's house. There are almost no pictures of him. Eve always got what she wanted, and she'd wanted my father. He'd been the ultimate trophy. Nothing on earth could convince me that love and attraction had been the reason he'd left a young, vibrant woman for a senior citizen who'd gone through menopause and had three adult children. She'd wanted a much younger man around so she could still feel attractive; he'd wanted a lifestyle of excess. It was a mutually beneficial union. Over the years, I couldn't help but wonder if they'd had sex, the thought horrifying. Like having sex with grandma.

In the kitchen, I unload the booty, put the jar of honey on the counter, and wash the apples. I can't find a cutting board, so I begin slicing fruit on a plate.

"What are you doing?" my dad asks from his seat at the kitchen table.

"Making an apple pie." I drop the slices into a glass pie pan.

"That's too much work," he says.

He and Eve didn't cook. The hired help cooked. The hired help shopped for groceries. The hired help made the beds and cleaned the house and washed the windows. But once the prime minister died, the alimony ended, and the days of maids and chefs vanished.

My dad goes quiet, thoughtful. "We're eating at the bar tonight, aren't we?" he asks after a little while. "I want you to come to the bar with me. I want you to see what my life is like."

Carol, the woman who takes care of him thirty hours a week, told me he goes to a place called Home Plate every night. I looked it up online before leaving St. Paul. A sports bar. I don't feel like dealing with the crowd and the noise, and I would like to see Dad get through one night without alcohol. His thinking degrades as the day wears on, and I suspect the booze. "Let's just stay in tonight, okay? That's why I'm baking this apple pie." I'm hoping the pie will be enough of a treat to convince him that we don't need to go to the bar. Even though I haven't been there, I can envision it in my head. "I'm not really crazy about sports bars," I tell him.

"It's not like that," he says. "They don't watch sports there."

"Are there televisions?"

"No. No televisions."

"Oh." Maybe I have the wrong idea. "Let's stay home tonight and go to Home Plate tomorrow."

I can see he doesn't like that idea. "I'm cooking chicken tacos," I tell him. "And I make a pretty decent apple pie." I finish with the crumble topping and stick the pie in the oven.

He keeps checking his watch. "I usually leave for the bar at five-thirty."

"How far is it from here?" I'm thinking it's probably a few blocks. It's reassuring to know he only drives to the bar and church.

"About six or seven miles."

It makes no sense that he would go so far to eat dinner, and I wonder if he's wrong about the distance. "We have to stay here. I just put a pie in the oven. We can go to the bar tomorrow."

"A pie?" he asks in surprise. "Were did that come from?"

"I made it."

"You *did*? Did you bring it with you?"

I picture myself running through the Atlanta airport with an apple pie in my hands. "I made it just now."

"You *did*?" He's baffled.

"Yes."

"What kind of pie?"

"Apple. You went with me to get the apples."

"Did we go to the grocery store?"

"No, we went to the fruit stand."

"Oh!" He looks at his watch, and his confusion falls away. "It's time to head to the bar."

"We can't leave. I just put a pie in the oven."

"Where did the pie come from? Did Carol bring it?"

"No, I made it."

"You *did*?" he says in fresh amazement, as if I just pulled an entire pie out of my ass.

Chapter 2

After dinner, my dad and I settle down in the sitting room. I'm in a chair that, with the push of a button, can slowly stand a person upright. Dad is in a recliner, a small table and lamp between us, a giant television screen in front of us. We spend an hour flipping through channels, and I begin to wish we'd gone to the bar. Occasionally Dad gets up to go to the kitchen, and every time he's amazed to find an apple pie on the counter.

Throughout the evening, I find my dad staring at me with a perplexed expression. Finally he comes right out and asks, "How are you related to me?"

"I'm your daughter."

He snaps his fingers. "I knew it!" He looks relieved to have figured it out. He's become a master at covering his memory loss, and he acts as if everyone he sees is a relative or good friend, even ones he can't remember. I suspect he's been doing that with me ever since I arrived last night.

"Do I have any other children?" he asks.

"You have two sons."

"Where do they live?"

"Idaho and Texas."

"How come I have no memories of any of you?"

Even if he didn't have Alzheimer's, he wouldn't have any memories of his children. I've seen him fewer than twenty times since he and my mother divorced fifty years ago, and all but a handful of those awkward and uncomfortable face-to-face encounters took place when I was an adult. I now realize that his larger return to my life coincided with his early symptoms of memory loss, which I suspect began when he was sixty. This meant he went undiagnosed for fifteen years.

I often imagine how his attempt at that more recent reconnection began. He may have been talking to a neighbor, and the neighbor mentioned her children. "They're coming to visit for the weekend," the neighbor tells my dad, then asks, "Do you have any kids?"

My dad thinks a moment. "Why, yes I do!"

"What are they like?" the neighbor asks, surprised because this is the first she's heard of any offspring. "They must live far away since I've never seen them. I'll bet they miss you. Will they be coming for Christmas?"

"I don't know if they're coming," Dad says, because his lack of a relationship with his children is his dirty little secret, tucked away and never spoken of.

"Well, Christmas will be here soon." The neighbor squeezes his arm. "Give them a call."

My dad remembers a phone number tucked away in the bottom of a drawer along with unanswered letters and school photos that eventually stopped coming. "I'll do that!" And he goes inside the house, has a couple of drinks, and makes the call.

This is how I imagine it happening. In those early stages of Alzheimer's, my father forgot that he wasn't like most fathers.

"We were never a part of your life," I tell him now.

"I wonder why." He becomes quiet, then finally says, "I was a bad person."

"You just had a different focus." I feel the need to give him reassurance, but not too much. "You cared about other things."

"Maybe I didn't care at all."

How, in this deep pit of confused memories and forgotten people, had he managed to find something so honest? Was it a fluke, just the dementia talking, or were these things he'd truly thought about or suppressed over the years, now surfacing even though he can no longer follow the thread? Before we can further explore the topic of his badness, his thoughts move on to memories and scenes that are often misplaced in the timeline of history, but vivid nonetheless. He recounts the same event several times in a row, and each time I act less interested, hoping he'll stop, yet feeling guilty for dampening his pleasure of the telling.

"I want to ask you something." My dad leans forward in his seat, elbows on his knees, head cocked in earnestness, and stares into my eyes. "What about your mother?"

I play along, acting as if I'm hearing this for the first time. "What do you mean?" I hope for answers and clues to a past that is probably lost to us both.

Questions I've heard a hundred times come at me again, one after the other: "Where does she live? How is she? What do you hear from her? Is she still beautiful? She used to be beautiful. Do you think she's still beautiful?"

"Probably not," I say. I know he's thinking of her at thirty, the way she was when he left her, pregnant with her third child. Shiny, raven hair, dark eyes, red lips. "She's old," I remind him.

"Some old people are still good looking."

I laugh at his wishful thinking, and I wonder at his obsession. It's not just my visits that trigger thoughts of my mother. When I'm home, he phones with questions of her, and with each call he presents the topic as if it just occurred to him for the first time in his life, something that happened to flit through his brain. Not a big deal.

But the number of times she comes up, the number of times in a single day that she is in his thoughts, tells a larger story. And now that a year has passed since Eve's death, he rarely talks about the woman on the wall above his head.

It's hard to know where his fixation with his first wife comes from. Guilt? Regret? Love? Loneliness?

"If you had her phone number, would you call her?" I ask.

"I wouldn't mind talking to her. I'd like to know how she's doing. I guess I'm curious about her."

This was more than idle curiosity. But to call her, to get in touch with her after all of these years ... He'd destroyed her. That's what he doesn't remember. She'd been a good mother until he abandoned her, and she never recovered. And I didn't have any information about her. Where she lived. What she looked like. "You know as much about her as I do," I tell him. I haven't seen her in over thirty years, not since the time I'd hemorrhaged after giving birth to my daughter. Doctors had struggled to control the blood loss, and my husband had called my parents.

"Why did you call my father?" I'd asked. He had nothing to do with me or my life. He didn't deserve to know anything about me, especially something as personal as dying.

"The doctors didn't know if you'd make it through the night," my husband had said. "I thought both of your parents should know."

When my mother heard about the phone call to the man who'd walked out on her, she never spoke to me again. At the time, I was surprised by how deeply betrayed she felt. By that point, she'd remarried, had a new life, but it took a long time for me to realize that she'd never gotten over my father.

When I was little she didn't hesitate to announce her hatred of him, loathing of him. She would sniff and say, "He's a stupid man, a crude man, with no appreciation for art or creativity." But I think she was crazy about him. That's what I think.

I have very few memories of the man sitting next to me. When I search my mind, when I pull up childhood events, birthdays, holidays, trips to the beach, he is never there. And because of lost relationships and now my father's lost mind, there is no one to ask, no way to find out the truth of my own past and the events that brought us both here. All I have are pieces, small, insignificant clips …

One of my few memories took place before the divorce. I was six years old, and I woke up to find my father and mother in bed, and they both seemed as happy as two sleepy kittens. He rarely slept or ate at our house, so it was a treat to see him. When he was around, my mother was lit from inside and I would bask in the glow. That Florida morning I crawled into bed with them, and they smiled at me with groggy laughter. My mother in her smudged mascara and lips that still held a trace of red that came from a gold tube. She was beautiful, and the joy she radiated filled the room. My father was happy too, but it wasn't the happiness of my mother. It was more of a smug happiness. He was living in the moment, and she was thinking about their lives together. Even at the age of six, I could sense the difference in their moods. And as they awakened, I felt the joy begin to seep from the room, to crawl out the door and down the hall, and out of the house as my father would soon do. He was not a part of our lives. He was the man who brought our mother happiness from time to time and then left. He always left.

I retrieved a book and squeezed between them, thinking that I might be able to make him stay if he knew I could read. But his praise quickly faded, and I saw boredom fill his eyes, and I recognized his need to be away from this place, away from us. We tried to hang on, we tried to coax him into our life, feed him small morsels that might tempt him, but we weren't enough. We could only make him happy for a short while. Something else called to him. A life we couldn't give him.

I'd bored him with the story. I closed the book and tried to hide it under the covers, hoping he would forget, hoping we could go back to the happiness of minutes ago, but it was too late.

"Can you stay?" I asked, unable to contain my anxiety.

"Yes, can you stay?" my mother echoed. "It's Sunday."

"I have to go." His hair was curly and black, his skin a deep brown against the white sheets. He worked on a fishing boat and was always outside. I compared my arm to his; it was almost as dark.

"We can go to the beach!" I would wear my blue swimsuit, black sunglasses, and carry my beach bag shaped like a watermelon. He would love it.

"I have to go." His face was now a face that scared me.

"Go get yourself some breakfast," my mother told me. Once I left, I heard the raised voices, the arguing that was followed by the slamming of the front door and sobs coming from the bedroom.

*

My elderly father sits and taps his fingers on the wooden arm of his recliner, his gaze returning to the clock on the wall. "Time for bed," he finally announces, sounding relieved that the next and final stage of his day has arrived.

The bedrooms are down a long narrow hall. The dogs join Dad in the master suite, and I take the room one door away.

There is no television and no Internet, and I wonder how in the world I will get to sleep. It's nine o'clock in Florida, but eight o'clock in St. Paul. I brought a book, but it doesn't hold my interest. The room is hot, and the bed feels hollow, with a dip in the center like a hammock.

If my dad doesn't know who I am during the day, how will he know in the middle of the night? He keeps a handgun in the drawer beside his bed, and Carol told me he threatened to shoot a neighbor's car, so Carol hid the bullets. This seems to be another of his obsessions. This irrational anger and a need to retaliate for some minor annoyance.

I lock the bedroom door and lie down, but my back hurts. I drag the mattress to the floor and place it between the twin beds. It just fits, but even though it feels a little firmer, squeezing between the beds is like lying in a coffin, the air stagnant, the carpet smelling like dust, mildew, and an old dog. The room belonged to a kid before my father moved here.

Light from the street cuts through the blinds, and I stare at the ceiling and wait for the night to end. I know I'm too old and my father is too damaged for me to feel the resentment I feel, but it's here and I can't ignore it.

People have asked me why I'm helping him, a man who erased his own children until we no longer existed.

"I don't know how you can forgive him," a friend said a few days earlier when we spoke on the phone.

I doubt I'll ever forgive him. It's not in me to forgive him, but my own sense of humanity won't let me ignore him and his plight. This would be easier if he were a stranger. Or if I loved him. If he were a stranger, I could help him without having to listen to stories that pierce my heart, stories of a fabulous life that didn't include his children. If I loved him, I would swoop him up and carry him off to live with me.

Through the wall, I hear him shift in his bed, and I hear the jingle of a dog collar, and I imagine the two Dalmatians curled beside him in the king-size bed. The walls are pale blue, covered in framed Irene Spencer prints—soft images of mothers cuddling babies. Long white dressers with gold trim are strewn with Eve's ornate perfume bottles and tiered glass shelves of jewelry. A floral spread covers my father in oblivion, his shape undefined and fragile. He doesn't know it, but he is the man who broke us.

Chapter 3

After the Divorce

Burlington, Iowa, 1961

"It will be a boarding house," my mother said, hands on hips, surveying the giant, three-story house from the steep front yard.

My baby brother had been born in June. A few weeks later we moved from Florida to Burlington, Iowa. Now, two months after arriving in the Midwest, we had a giant stone house as big as a castle, and my mother had opened a maternity shop a few blocks away, in a brick building that had once been a market. I liked our big, spooky house. It had long hallways of doors, wooden floors, and creepy metal lights that hung from high ceilings. The whole house echoed, and our furniture looked tiny and wrong. There were so many bedrooms, some downstairs, even more on the second and third floors. Above the third level was a turret where my older brother and I found a Candy Land game. The box was old and dusty, so maybe kids had lived there a long time ago. Maybe they were grown-ups now.

We could choose our bedrooms, and my big brother and I picked rooms on the second story. Our mother chose the first floor, putting a crib in one corner. "When the house fills with boarders you'll have to move downstairs," she warned.

"Will they eat with us?" I asked. I didn't like that idea. Somebody I didn't know, eating at our table.

"We'll all share the same kitchen, but we probably won't eat together."

I was relieved to hear that. The idea of sharing with strangers made me uncomfortable.

The house was okay, but I'd come for the snow and I was still waiting.

My mother told me there would be no snow in June, but I hoped she was wrong. I'd been around long enough to learn that she didn't know everything.

"I miss Florida," I told my mother one morning as we ate breakfast, boxes of cereal on the table. My older brother, Thomas, was away at an uncle's. He was away a lot.

"How could you miss that awful place?" she asked. "Florida was awful. Just awful. The bugs! Have you forgotten the bugs? And hurricanes! The hurricanes were horrible!"

"There are tornadoes here." I'd heard the sirens, and I'd seen girls running down the sidewalk, screaming.

"I'd rather have a tornado than a hurricane," she said. "Huddled in a dark house for days, no electricity. I never want to do that again."

"I liked it." And when the wind had stopped and the eye of the hurricane was overhead, we'd all run outside to marvel at the silence.

I missed the smell of the ocean and the palm trees and the sun and the light-colored buildings. Everything in Iowa was dark, even the Mississippi River. Just brown, swirling water that smelled like rotten things.

"Where's the river?" I'd asked, looking across the dark water to the trees on the other side. "I want to see the Mississippi." In Florida, my mother had talked a lot about the Mississippi River, and I couldn't wait to see it. And she'd read *Tom Sawyer* and *Huck Finn* to us.

"This *is* the river," she'd said.

I stared. "Is it ever clear? Is it ever blue?"

"It's called the muddy Mississippi."

"Do people swim in it?" I tried to imagine putting my face in the dirty water.

"Of course they do."

"I don't think I want to."

And the fish! Nothing beautiful. No blue marlins or sailfish. No starfish or stingrays or barracudas or swordfish. The Mississippi River had catfish. I liked the name and had been anxious to see one, but a catfish ended up being small and slimy, with a wide, ugly mouth and whiskers that would sting if you touched them.

In Iowa, gray clouds got tangled in tree branches, and rain never seemed to stop hitting my bedroom window. In Iowa, the stars weren't as close, and when I spread a blanket on the lawn and looked up at the night sky, I couldn't find Sputnik, the Russian satellite.

"There's no Castro here," my mother said. At school in Florida, we'd had weekly drills where we learned to crawl under our desks.

"How far away is he?" I asked.

"Thousands of miles."

"So he won't drop a bomb on this house?"

"No."

"Couldn't he shoot a bomb this far?"

"He's not smart enough." My mother got up from the table to put dishes in the sink. "Just wait until the snow comes," she said over her shoulder. "You'll love it here then. You can go sledding and make a snowman."

"And snow angels?"

"And snow angels."

I was waiting for snow, and my mother was waiting for my father to come back. It was just a matter of time, she said. She kept their wedding album on the coffee table in front of the couch, and she and I looked at it every day. I particularly liked the photo of my dad walking down the aisle with my mother holding his arm. He was winking to someone who wasn't in the picture.

"Who's he winking at?" I always asked, hoping my mother would remember.

"I don't know."

They were both so happy, and the photo album made me feel good and reminded me of what we would once again have. My father would get tired of the old, boring woman, and he would come back to us. The wedding album, with its place of importance in the center of the living room, was a promise that was made every time I passed it, every time I looked at it, every time I opened it.

"I talked to your father last night," my mother told me one day. I could see the old joy in her face, and a smile hovered near the corner of her mouth. I could feel her excitement. "I think he's coming back to us," she said.

"I bounced on her bed. I wanted to run into the living room and get the wedding album. "Will we move to Florida? Will he move here? Is he tired of the old lady?"

My mother laughed, and it was a real laugh, one I hadn't heard in a long time. "I'm trying to talk him into coming here, to Iowa."

"When?"

"I don't know. Soon, maybe. But don't say anything to anybody else. Not until I know for sure."

She shared a lot of things with me, things I couldn't tell anyone else, not even my older brother. I ran to get the wedding album. I'd looked at it so many times the pages were beginning to come loose. I plopped on the floor and opened it to the first page. "But he said he was coming?"

"I asked him if he'd think about coming back, and he said yes."

"Yes!" On my stomach, I braced a hand under my chin, my knees bent, feet in the air, and went through the album one picture at a time.

Chapter 4

Our first and only boarder was an eighteen-year-old girl named Monica. She'd been in "trouble," and had been sent away to another town to have a baby. Now she was back without the baby, working part time at a jewelry counter in a downtown store. Not long after she moved into our house, she started watching the maternity shop a few afternoons a week. She had shiny blond hair, pale skin, and big green eyes. She looked like a movie star. Right away she invited me to her room at the front of the house on the second floor. I wasn't used to anybody her age paying attention to me, and before long I found myself waiting for her to get home from work. I always expected her to ignore me, but as soon as she stepped inside she would invite me upstairs. We'd run to her room where we'd sit on the bed and listen to records while she painted my nails and put curlers in my hair. We talked about movies and actors and boys.

"You can be my little sister," she told me one afternoon as she capped a jar of nail polish. "I've always wanted a sister."

I ducked my head and blew on my red nails, afraid to let her see how happy I was. I wanted my curly hair to be straight like hers, and I wanted my Florida tan to fade faster.

She got up to put the nail polish away. From my seat on the bed, I watched her light a cigarette, then drop the lighter on the dresser.

She saw me watching her. "Would you like a cigarette?" she asked, blowing smoke at the ceiling.

I pressed my hands to my face, giggled, and nodded. I'd put my mother's unlit cigarettes in my mouth, pretending to smoke, but I'd never tried to light one.

Monica shook her head. "You're too young. Maybe when you're older. I have to watch out for my little sister."

On the dresser behind her was a large wooden jewelry box. She lifted it with both hands and carried it to the bed, cigarette between her fingers. "Pick out one piece of jewelry," she said.

"To wear for fun?"

"To keep, silly. Go on. Open it."

I opened the box. It was like a treasure chest. Sparkling jewelry spilled out. Everything was shiny colored glass. Or diamonds. Maybe they were diamonds.

"How come you have so much jewelry?" I asked.

"I get a discount at work, and sometimes they even give me free jewelry."

"I can pick anything?"

"Anything."

It took me a while to decide between earrings that looked like shells and a blue necklace. I finally chose the necklace. I put it around my neck and Monica hooked the clasp. I wore it the rest of the afternoon while we talked and played cards and listened to records. Later, while I colored, she wrote letters to people I didn't know, and I licked the envelopes and stamps for her. After Monica left for work, I kept the necklace on, and I wore it to the dinner table that night.

"Where did you get that?" my mother asked from her seat across the table. The baby was in her arms, patting the bottle of milk held to his mouth while he watched me with big blue eyes that never seemed to blink.

"Monica gave it to me."

She frowned, leaned forward, and fingered the shiny glass beads. "Give it back."

"Why?"

"You can't accept a gift like that from someone you hardly know."

"I know her."

"You can't keep it. And anyway, it's tacky. It's not a kid's necklace. It's like something that woman might own."

"The old lady?"

"Yes. It's just the kind of glittering, showy, tacky necklace she would wear. I don't want to see it on you again. And take off that ridiculous nail polish. You look like a streetwalker."

My older brother laughed, batted his eyelashes, and made kissing noises at me.

The next day, I tried to return the necklace. "My mom says I can't keep it," I told Monica. We were in her room again. She was lying in bed with her back against the headboard, blowing smoke rings at the ceiling, an ashtray balanced on her stomach. She wore white slacks that stopped above her ankles, and her feet were bare, her toenails red.

She put the ashtray and cigarette aside and sat up straight, her eyes flashing. "I can give you a present if I want to! Your mother can't tell me what to do."

I pushed the necklace toward her across the bedspread. "Here." I didn't want her mad at me.

Monica slipped the necklace on me. I looked down and thought about the old lady and her jewelry. The necklace didn't seem pretty anymore. I wished Monica hadn't given it to me.

"It's a gift from me to you," Monica said. "Your mother can't keep me from giving you a present."

"She said *no*."

"Don't tell her about it. It'll be our secret. You can wear it when you come to my room. I'll keep it in the jewelry box, and you can take it out and wear it when you're here."

"Okay." I liked that idea. Everything was fine, and I adored her.

*

"I think Monica is stealing from me," my mother said one day when Monica was away from our house. "There are never any sales when she's watching the shop."

"Maybe nobody is going to the store," I said. Monica wouldn't steal. The idea made me feel sick and confused. My mother had to be wrong. She was wrong about a lot of things. She said I'd like it in Iowa, and I didn't. She said I wouldn't miss Florida or my father, but I did. She said he would come back to us, and so far that hadn't happened. She said a lot of people would want to rent rooms in our house, but Monica was the only person living with us.

"We'll see. Come on." My mother bundled baby Jude. "We're going to be secret agents. We're going to spy on Monica. It'll be fun."

I didn't believe that either.

We got in the car and drove toward the shop, stopping down the block. We could see the front door. As we watched, a car pulled up and a woman got out and went inside. Fifteen minutes later, she came back with a pink box under her arm.

"Sale," my mother said with satisfaction.

We waited until another customer came and went, this one also carrying a box. Then we drove home. Being secret agents *was* fun.

That afternoon, after the shop closed, Monica returned.

"Any customers?" my mother asked innocently, a cup of coffee in her hands.

I stood on a chair at the kitchen counter and poured sugar into my cup of coffee, then stirred it with a spoon while waiting for Monica to show my mother the money she'd made that day.

"Dead," Monica said. "Not a single person."

My mother made a *tsk, tsk* sound with her tongue. "I just don't get it," she said. "There never seem to be any customers on the afternoons you work. Isn't that strange?"

Monica shrugged. "It does seem weird I guess."

Oh, what a good actress she was! Even though I knew the truth, even though I knew she was lying, I almost believed her. I wanted to believe her. I took a sip of coffee, hoping it would taste like chocolate. It never did, but I drank it anyway.

"I'm going to report her to the police," my mother told me later that day after Monica left for the department store and jewelry counter. "But first I have to prove that she's pocketing money. I have to figure out what dresses are gone, and how much she sold them for. And I'll bet you anything that necklace she gave you was stolen."

"What will the police do?"

"They'll arrest her. They'll throw her in jail where she belongs."

That night, I couldn't sleep. I kept picturing the police coming to the door and putting handcuffs on Monica, then taking her away. The next morning, after my mother left for the shop, taking the baby with her, I tapped on Monica's door.

She let me in, and I told her. About the women and the boxes and my mother's suspicions and the police.

"It's all a lie!" she said.

I wanted to believe her, but I'd been in the car. I'd seen the women leaving the shop. But still … Maybe there was an explanation. A lot of things that happened never made sense to me. Adults could sometimes explain them, but not always.

She began throwing clothes in a suitcase.

I stared. "Are you leaving?" I didn't think she'd leave. I thought she'd explain. I thought she'd say she'd given both ladies empty boxes for some reason. Or they'd bought something earlier and had come back to get it.

"I'm sure as hell not staying around here when your mother is accusing me of stealing!" She was nervous. In a hurry. She seemed different. Not the

Monica I knew. This one was intense and hard. Had I done the right thing? Should I have told her?

In five minutes she was packed.

She shoved the necklace into my hands. "It's yours. I gave it to you. Just hide it so your mom doesn't see it."

"Where will you go?" I thought about the letters she was always writing.

"No idea. But don't tell your mother I've left. Let her find out for herself, okay? Promise?"

"Promise."

"Will you write?"

"I suppose I could send you something with no return address, but your mother would catch on. I'd better not."

"She said the necklace is stolen too. It's not stolen, is it?"

"Of course not! How can you say such a thing?"

She was uncomfortable. I don't think it was as easy for her to lie to me. Or maybe she didn't try as hard.

I watched her leave. Watched her head out the door and down the front steps, her arms full of suitcases, large and small. I didn't know where she was going, but I wanted to go with her.

She loaded the suitcases in the trunk of her dented green car with the silver stripe, looking up and down the street, her shoulders hunched as if trying to hide. She scurried behind the steering wheel, starting the car before the driver's door was closed. And then in a cloud of exhaust and grinding of gears, Monica was gone.

The blue necklace was still in my hand. I went inside and up to my room, where I hid the jewelry in the back of a drawer, behind my underwear.

Monica hadn't been with us long, but I already missed her.

Our life in Florida had been magic. And even though I was just a kid, I could feel the wrongness here, the sadness. Monica had brought light into our darkness, a sense of excitement about tomorrow. With her talk of boys and movie stars, her music and her painted toe nails. Things that didn't matter, and yet they did. Now that she was gone, the house felt dark again. I didn't understand the darkness, but I knew it came from my mother. You could see it in the air, and feel it creeping around the corners, crawling into cracks. It was in the bathroom and in the kitchen cupboards. And when we left the house, it followed us. It rode in the car beside me, and it took my hand in the grocery store. Even my shoes were sad. Monica had changed that. She'd broken through the sadness for a little while. But now it was back. I could feel it again, sneaking up the stairs, crawling under the door to my room.

I didn't think my mother would find out that I'd warned Monica. I don't know how she knew, but that night she came raging into my room, asking questions. Within a minute, I was blabbing.

"How could you?" my mother said. "How could you do that to me?"

"I didn't want her to go to jail."

"Now I'll never get the money she stole, do you realize that? Do you understand what you've done? And not only did she get away with the money she stole from the shop, she owes me a month's rent! I wanted to help her. All I wanted to do was help her."

My mother liked to help people. In Florida, she'd brought one of her students home from the Catholic school. She'd washed and cut the girl's matted hair, and screamed when bugs ran down her arms. She'd given the girl new clothes, and clucked over her bruised legs.

The girl had shrugged. "My father beats me with an extension cord."

My mother had been horrified.

"I was helping Monica," I said. "She was my friend."

"She wasn't your friend. She used you."

"I didn't want her to go to jail," I repeated.

"So you betrayed me? Your mother? In order to protect that little conniving slut? You chose her over me?"

Had I?

"You're just like your father. She bought you, just like that pig in Florida bought your dad. "You can bet I'll never tell you any secrets, anything I don't want the rest of the world to know." She was in a rage, and spit flew from her mouth. "I should send you to live with him. That's what I should do. Is that what you want? To go live with your dad and his pig? Swim in her pool? Ride in her Rolls Royce?"

She could see I was thinking about it, wondering if it might be okay.

"You can't live with him! He didn't want us anymore!"

"But he's coming back. You said he was coming back."

My words startled her, but she quickly came around, this time a little subdued. "Stay in your room.

I don't want to see your face downstairs." She slammed the door.

My older brother seemed to live to cause trouble, and up until now I'd been the good kid. Up until now, I'd always done what I was told to do. If I spotted my older brother involved in something questionable, I felt it was my duty to sound the alarm. But I finally understood why my brother was always doing things he shouldn't do. It felt kind of good.

I hadn't been able to stop my father from leaving us, and I hadn't been able to keep us from moving from Florida, or keep Monica from stealing, or stop the sadness from creeping in, but I'd rescued Monica. I'd kept her from going to jail.

Chapter 5

My grandmother arranged for my brothers and me to travel with her to California, where my dad and the old lady now lived. For some reason, my dad and Eve had left Florida and moved across the country to Los Angeles. My mother said it was so they could live together without the old lady's ex-husband finding out. I didn't understand it, but Eve got a lot of money from him as long as she stayed single.

My grandmother paid for our tickets, and she somehow convinced Dad, someone we hadn't seen or heard from in years, to allow us to visit him. I guess he couldn't say no when his mother was paying for the trip. So we were on our way to California, and I was terrified and excited at the thought of seeing my father again after so many years. The hardest part had been convincing our mother to let us go. That summer she finally gave us permission as long as we understood that we were going as spies. And we were not to have a good time. This was a mission. A job. To observe and report back. And to cause chaos, misery, and embarrassment while we were there. I could do that. All three of us could do that.

On the day of our departure, we got up early, when the sky was still black, and drove to Ft. Madison, Iowa, to catch the Chief, the Amtrak train that ran across the country and would eventually drop us off in Los Angeles, California. The trip would take two nights and three days, and, as I understood it, we were allowed to enjoy the train ride. No need to spy or report any of the events that took place before stepping on California soil. No need to talk of the meals eaten in the dining car while the train moved through the countryside, the waiter swaying with amazing balance. No need to talk about playing cards in the observation car, or reading books under the overhead light. No need to share the story of Grandma snoring loudly through the night, and how she made us put on pajamas to sleep in seats that didn't recline enough to lie down. It would have been okay to share these things with my mother, but the train adventure wasn't what she wanted to hear about. The train wasn't our mission.

As we neared the station in California, my stomach began to hurt. And by the time the train stopped and we were fighting the steps with our heavy suitcases, I felt like I might throw up.

In the bright sun, we scanned the crowd, looking for my father and the old lady. Would I recognize him? Did I even want to see him? Would he recognize us? He'd never even met my baby brother, who was now four.

Suddenly a man moved forward out of the shade, leaving behind a woman dressed in a beige suit and pearls.

My father was smaller than I remembered, and I experienced a small pang of disappointment. His clothes weren't what I'd expected, a pale blue shirt with square tails, and white slacks with a sharp crease. Pale, slip-on shoes with tassels. I didn't remember him in such things, and I knew that these changes were because of her. But when he spoke, the voice was the same. Everything else was different, but the voice took me back to those happy times in Florida when we were a family.

He didn't hug any of us, not even his mother. Instead, he busied himself collecting what suitcases he could carry, and we got the rest. I grasped the handle of my suitcase with both hands and leaned as I walked. We followed him to the shade and the old lady.

I'd seen her before. In Florida, but it had been from a distance, like some woman in a magazine waving an elegant arm from the beautiful doorway of her mansion. This was our first face-to-face. I'd imagined her looking old, like the crone who lived down the street from us. But she was dressed in clothes that smelled like perfume and a steam iron, and her hair was perfect, with one big white wave against golden brown. Her long fingernails were shiny red, and her arms and hands moved with an elegance that tricked me, that made me think she was beautiful when she was actually unattractive once you got past the hair and jeweled glasses and red, red lips. When she spoke, it was like hearing someone on television, someone in a movie. I think she had an English accent, but I wasn't sure. I would work hard to imitate it before we went home.

I stared as I tried to memorize everything about her.

"She's had two facelifts," my mother had told me. But now, looking at the old lady, I didn't see how that could be true, because chunks of sagging skin hung on either side of her wrinkled mouth.

Adults were easy to read, and I felt annoyance coming from her; yet at the same time, she bent slightly at the knees and leaned forward in front of my older brother. He stared, a puzzled expression on his face. "Hi," he finally said.

Her eyes flashed in irritation as she gave up on him and presented herself to me in the same manner. I think I was supposed to kiss her. With hesitation, I leaned forward and quickly touched my lips to her cheek. Her skin was soft, like a marshmallow. I thought I was done when she turned her face, presenting the other cheek and I was forced to do the same. I came away smelling like perfume, powder, and the old lady.

Thomas had escaped the greeting, but now that I'd figured out the expected behavior, my younger brother and grandmother followed my lead. I wished I'd just said hi, too. It was like we were all being blessed by the queen. I wondered what I should call her. Certainly not Mom. Maybe, *Your Majesty.* The thought made me giggle to myself. I wished I had the nerve, but I didn't. That was the kind of thing my brothers would do, not me. I would suggest it to Jude later on.

Eve. I guess I would call her Eve.

In the car, her fingernails tap, tap, tapped as we drove to the place they lived, my dad behind the wheel, the old lady in front, my baby brother between them, chattering like a magpie. When he was excited he didn't shut up. My grandmother, older brother, and I filled the backseat, giving me a good opportunity to observe what was going on in front of me.

"The two older children look like you," Eve told my father. "But this one—" A slight movement of her head indicated she was talking about my younger brother. "Where did you get that blond hair?" she asked my brother.

It was a common question that my mother always explained by telling people her side of the family had a little Swede in them.

"Not from him!" Jude pointed to Dad and laughed. That was also part of the joke, but now, sitting in the car with Dad, it didn't seem quite so funny as it did when our mother told it.

"He doesn't have any of his father in him, thank God," she'd say. "He doesn't look or act at all like him."

"Does anybody in your family have straight blond hair?" Eve asked. "And those blue eyes …"

Thomas and I had eyes the color of dark chocolate. And our hair looked just like Dad's, dark and curly. Our skin, which was kind of olive, didn't even look like Jude's.

"Not that I know of," Dad said.

"Didn't you have a deckhand with hair this very color? What was his name?"

Beside me, my grandmother stiffened.

"Jerry," my dad finally said.

"Yes, that was it." Eve nodded. "Regardless, I don't think you should feel any obligation to this boy."

I didn't understand. I looked at my older brother. Did he know what they were talking about? He had a smirk on his face. But then something outside distracted him, and he pressed his face to the window. "Look. Smog!" He pointed to tall buildings surrounded by a thick haze.

I could smell it. Within five minutes, my throat and eyes burned, and my head began to ache. I sighed. I'd hoped California would be like Florida, but it wasn't.

Thirty minutes later, we arrived at a house that looked like a motel.

I could still feel Eve's annoyance. Maybe it wasn't us. Maybe she wasn't used to being around kids. My mother told me that her own children, now adults, had gone to boarding school. Maybe she wasn't used to noise and chatter, and could my baby brother chatter.

"Hurry," Eve said. "Hurry inside."

Before my father opened the front door, I heard dogs barking on the other side, deep barks, followed by the click of toenails.

They were the ugliest dogs I'd ever seen. "What are they?" I asked, as their drool trailed over my hands and legs.

"Basset Hounds," my father said.

"They're show dogs," the old lady informed me.

She didn't seem at all annoyed by the noisy, slobbering dogs. She loved them up and sweet-talked them, and even let them lick her mouth when she bent down to tell them hello.

I pulled my tablet from my white plastic purse, clicked my pen, and wrote:

She looks like her dogs. My mother would be happy to know this.

If I had a camera, I would take pictures of the old lady and the dogs and put them side by side. I would have felt bad about making such a mean observation, but I could already tell she wasn't a nice person. She wasn't one of those old ladies you wanted to hang out with unless you liked to hang out with old ladies who baked kids in ovens or served razor-blade apples.

"She might not be quite so homely if she wasn't dressed in rags, darling."

It took me a moment to realize Eve was talking to my dad about me.

She made a sour face. "Does your ex-wife think we're idiots? Making these poor children wear clothes from a thrift store to make us look bad?" This explained why she'd shooed us inside so quickly. Before the neighbors could see us. She made direct eye contact with me. "Where are your real clothes?" she demanded.

"What real clothes?" I didn't understand.

"Oh, come now. Admit the trick. You can tell us. Your real clothes were left behind and replaced with trash to embarrass us."

"These *are* my real clothes." I stared at her jowls. I imagined a doctor pulling at them, stretching them, cutting them off and sewing up her face. *Lifting* her face. Well, they'd better lift it a whole lot more.

"Don't lie, dear."

"I'm not lying. These are my best clothes. My very best clothes." I'd spent two weeks getting ready for the trip. Right now I was wearing a top that I'd made out of two large and beautiful nylon handkerchiefs. Around my waist was a woven belt. The outfit was completed with cutoffs that stopped at mid-thigh, and a pair of sneakers that had once been white, but were now kind of brown and had holes in the toes. My grandmother had gotten the purse for me.

"You didn't bring anything better than what you're wearing?" Eve asked.

I shook my head.

She turned to my father and said, "That ex-wife of yours wants them to come home with new wardrobes. What a sneak. She knew we couldn't be seen in public with them looking like homeless beggars. You'll have to take them shopping. Get one outfit and make them wear it the entire time. Serves them right for pulling such a trick."

How she twisted things. Had she told my father just such lies about my mother? I waited for him to defend me, to tell her I wouldn't lie, but he didn't. Instead, he looked ashamed and embarrassed, like a kid who'd been caught hanging out with the unpopular crowd. He shot me an angry frown and said he'd take me shopping tomorrow.

I was used to a person's expression matching the words that were being spoken, but Eve said awful things in a soft voice while smiling sweetly. It was like watching a ventriloquist's dummy that smiled while saying horrible things. To lessen the sting, she added words like darling and sweetheart to the end of her sentences, as if those words could trick a person into thinking she'd just said something nice. I think it worked for my dad. Or did he just pretend to believe her? Did he go along with whatever she wanted so he could stay here? So she wouldn't kick him out?

I pulled out my notebook and wrote: *She's just like the evil stepmother in Cinderella. But instead of three daughters, she has three sons.*

My brothers and I were given a room on the second floor. The house was so big I got lost, and everything was covered with soft, white carpet. In the bedroom, I unpacked my clothes and hung them in the closet. The hangers weren't regular hangers; they were padded with white satin fabric and each one probably cost more than the clothes in my suitcase. I was about to close the closet door when a cardboard box caught my eye.

I knew I shouldn't be snooping, but I looked closer. Dad's address was on the top, written in black magic marker. It was the box we'd sent him last Christmas. The outside was covered in stickers, little green wreathes and red stockings, things we'd added before giving the package to my mother to mail. She hadn't been happy about it, and I'd always wondered if she'd sent it. I was glad to see that she had. And glad to see that Dad had saved the box. Maybe it meant something to him.

What did he keep in it now?

I lifted one of the flaps and spotted Christmas paper. I opened the box completely—and saw that the gifts were just as we'd packed them, all there, all unopened. Even the construction-paper cards were still sealed. I felt both hurt and ashamed. I wanted to take back the cheap trinkets and homemade crafts. I wanted to throw away the unworthy presents.

How many days until we went home? I wanted to go home.

"You can hang your clothes in the closet," Eve had told me as she threw open the bedroom door and showed me my room. I think she did it on purpose. I think she'd wanted me to find the box.

*

The next morning my father was gone before we got up, but the old lady was home. The kitchen table had been set, and each place had stacks of plates and two glasses that looked like something my mother might use for wine. In the center of the stacked plates was half of a grapefruit.

I was hungry, so I sat down and started digging at it.

"Stop," Eve commanded. "You don't eat until everyone is at the table." Once we'd all taken a seat, she gave me a lesson: "This is a grapefruit spoon," Eve said. She demonstrated how it was used. It took forever, but I finally finished my fruit and got to my feet to go out and look at the pool. All that for a piece of grapefruit.

"Sit down," Eve commanded.

I sat.

Two girls in maid uniforms poured water and orange juice, another poured coffee for Eve and my grandmother. And then a big man in a white chef's jacket appeared and stood to one side of the room, hands clasped below his waist.

"I'll have two eggs over-easy and two slices of bacon," Eve told him. "What kind of bread have you baked today?"

"Blueberry muffins and banana bread, ma'am."

"I'll have both. And Sofia, where is the morning paper?"

The girl hurried off.

I stared at my plate. If I looked at my brothers, I would start laughing. I didn't know why it was so funny. It was just so weird, so unnecessary. Such an ordeal. At home, I shoved food in my mouth—if I could find any—and ran out the door.

"I'll have the same thing," my grandmother said. She was uncomfortable, and I wondered why we'd come; I wondered what we were doing here. This wasn't fun. Maybe it would get fun, but it wasn't fun now.

"You can have whatever you fancy," Eve told her as she unfolded a white cloth napkin and spread it across her lap.

"I don't want you to go to any extra trouble," Grandma told the chef.

He smiled and glanced at Eve. "I don't mind. That's what I'm here for."

Grandma got flustered. "Eggs and bacon are fine."

The chef looked at me. "And what about you, miss? What would you like?"

I stared at him. He was the blackest man I'd ever seen in my life. I wondered where he lived. I wondered if he was married. I wondered if he had kids. I imagined them living in a pink house with palm trees and maybe strings of happy lights and fun music. Did his kids ever come here? Did they ever swim in the pool? Did the chef hate Eve?

"How about pancakes?" he suggested. "How about a nice stack of blueberry pancakes with maple syrup?"

I was salivating already. I nodded, and looked back down at the grapefruit. How foolish I'd been to think it was all we were getting. Tomorrow I would know better. Tomorrow I would be prepared.

I tried to think of how to tell my mother about this. She would laugh at the extravagance, but I also had the feeling it might make her mad.

"What did the ghost say to the bee," my younger brother asked Eve.

"I don't know. What?"

"Boo, bee!"

He collapsed in a fit of giggles while Eve acted as if he'd never spoken.

I didn't know what was funnier: the silly joke, my brother's giggles, or Eve's reaction. Another thing for my notebook and we weren't even done with breakfast.

*

My father was always gone when we got up, and Eve always left after breakfast. I wasn't sure what they did all day, but I was told Eve owned several businesses in the area, and they also had lunch engagements. Maybe they just wanted to avoid hanging out with us. My grandmother was afraid to drive in the city, so we spent the days alone in the big house playing cards and swimming in the pool. I was just glad when Eve and my father were gone and I didn't have to watch everything I said or did.

One day a beautiful woman with dark hair stopped by looking for my father.

"I had no idea Warren had children," she said. She wore pearls around her neck and a skinny black dress that seemed too fancy for daytime. She wanted to know all about us, and when Eve came home and heard of the woman's visit, she didn't like it. My dad seemed flattered.

"I don't know why she stopped by," Eve said.

I was eager to help with that question. "She said she thought Dad might need somebody to wash his back."

Eve muttered something about socialite trash and stomped away. Later I heard her and my dad arguing. "You might think it's funny," Eve said, "but she's broken up two marriages and I don't want her in this house." Just what my mother had said about Eve. Apparently Eve wasn't the only woman who thought it was okay to go after a man when he was with another woman. It seemed to be the accepted thing with rich people.

One evening we went out to eat, not to some fancy restaurant with tablecloths, but a pizza place with long wooden tables. The waitress passed us our menus. "So what do you have going on tonight?" she asked my father.

"My mother is visiting us from Iowa," he said.

Iowa suddenly seemed a far-away, embarrassing place where all the men and women wore bib overalls and chewed on blades of grass. Sitting here in the coolness of California, I didn't want to be from Iowa.

"That's nice." The waitress looked around the table and zeroed in on Eve. "Are you enjoying your visit?"

The room became icy and Eve sat up straighter. "I'm not his mother." She should have been used to people thinking she was Dad's mom, or even his grandmother.

I opened my plastic purse and pulled out my tablet to take notes.

"Dear, you must be new." Eve's voice took on a kind, confiding tone as she spoke to the young girl in the red checkered uniform. "The wait staff's position is that of a servant," Eve told the girl. "You should never engage in personal conversation with the customers. You must remember your station."

The teenager stood there for a few seconds, lips trembling. Then she burst into tears and ran away. I saw her behind the counter sharing what had just occurred with the cook and two servers. Several pairs of eyes looked our way, and mouths dropped open.

Poor girl," Eve said in a sad voice. "I really hated to do that, but of course it had to be done." She sighed as if she'd just performed an unpleasant duty. "Warren, darling. Don't leave the girl a tip. She has to learn, and hopefully this will be a lesson for her."

Oh how easy it was for her to turn everything around!

"She's just a young high-school girl," my grandmother said. "This is probably a summer job for her, a way to make a little extra money. I don't see any harm in what she did. She was just trying to be friendly. And shoot, who cares? We *are* the same age." Grandma laughed, but I could tell from the way she was fiddling with her water, her ring tapping the glass with each turn, that she was upset.

"She should be doing something else," Eve said. "Babysitting, not waiting tables if she doesn't know proper decorum."

To entertain myself while we waited for pizza, I drew stick people on my tablet; one was Eve and one was the waitress. The waitress held a pizza over Eve's head, and the bubble by the waitress's mouth said, "How did you say you wanted your pizza?" Keeping the notebook below the tabletop, I passed it to my older brother who made another bubble and a line to Eve's mouth. "Please place the crown of pizza on my head, you bad waitress."

We both thought the drawing was hilarious even though it really wasn't very funny.

We didn't see the waitress again, and one of the cooks brought our pizzas and silently placed them on the table. Eve seemed pleased with herself, and I hoped the chef hadn't poisoned us.

I would have found the evening entertaining if not for the waitress and her tears. I wondered if she would quit because of Eve. Maybe she'd go home and throw herself on her bed, hug a stuffed animal, cry, and tell her mother she couldn't go back to work the next day, all because of some horrible, mean woman.

This person sitting across from me was the reason my father had left us. This mean, nasty, old person. And she wasn't even interesting. Some mean people were interesting and fun, even if they were mean. I had an uncle like that. But if you took away the mean and the old and the ugly and the graceful hand movements and the accent, she would be nothing. She would be a potato with a heartbeat.

Was it all about the giant house and servants? Was it all about white carpet and drinks from fancy glasses? All along I'd clung to the idea that Eve must have had something interesting about her, something compelling that mere weak men couldn't resist. Because, after all, my dad had married my mother, and it would have been hard to find a person more interesting than Mom even if she did throw hairbrushes. And what about the dark-haired woman who'd stopped by the house to see my father? What about her?

In the bustle of leaving, my grandmother slipped some bills under her plate and winked at me. That gave me an idea. I opened my purse, tore out the picture I'd drawn, and left it on the table. I hoped the waitress found it. Maybe it would make her laugh.

When we left California, I think everybody was relieved except my little brother. He'd had a good time, and he was too young to feel the weird undercurrents. He'd loved the swimming pool, and he'd loved the food, and he'd loved the house. He'd loved asking my dad for a cocktail in a pompous voice, adding darling to the end, and he'd loved the time he'd pushed a visiting friend's daughter in the pool even though he'd been spanked and sent to his room without supper. He'd been our hero that night. Not to be outdone, Thomas wrote EVE IS A BITCH in giant letters in the sludge at the deep end of the pool shortly before we left. It had taken him quite a while, and he'd had to dive several times. Once it was done, it could be seen from the upstairs bedrooms.

We returned to Iowa to find that our mother had given away our dog while we were gone.

"That's what you get for going to California," she said in a matter o' fact voice.

"Is he at the pound?" I asked, crying. The pound was the place where most of our animals went. "We can go get him. Let's go get him right now."

"I didn't take him to the pound."

"Where is he? We have to get him back!"

"I don't know where he is," she said. "Some nice man was walking by and asked if he could have him. I didn't get his name, and I don't know where he lives."

I kept watch, hoping the nice man would walk by with our dog. But I never saw him, and after two weeks I felt stupid for believing my mother. There was no man. She'd taken the dog to the pound. She hadn't wanted me to find him there. And now it was too late. He had either been adopted or put to sleep.

That's what you get for going to California.

At first, my brothers and I didn't talk about the trip. But my mother wanted to know every detail of Dad and Eve's lives. She roared with us when we told the story of the pizza place and how the waitress thought Eve was Dad's mother. She laughed when we told her Eve's dogs looked just like Eve. She relished the tales of the young, gorgeous woman who came by the house.

"He won't be with Eve much longer," my mother said. "Soon he'll be someone else's boy toy."

"Maybe your boy toy," I said. It was a joke, meant to make her laugh.

"I'm too poor. He'll move on to someone richer than Eve. And if he can't find anybody with more money, he'll stay with her. That's what I think."

"But she's old."

My mother smiled a grim smile. "Yes, she is. And she's had cancer. She only has one breast, you know. She's an aging socialite with one boob." And then she laughed for real.

We were spies, and our mother wanted to know what they talked about, and what they ate, and how they dressed. How big the house was, where it was located. An expensive part of L. A., she decided. What with the view of the city and the size of the lot.

I learned to leave out anything that might have been fun, and whenever she begged for a rerun of events, I was careful to make it all sound horrible and stupid and boring. And most of it was, but their lifestyle had also been a curiosity to me. But when I told her about Eve saying she'd deliberately sent us there in rags … that set her off. And we were suddenly two girls sharing our outrage.

I told her how they got drunk in the early evening, and how Eve would slump against my father and call him my sweets, and dear heart, and darling.

Sometimes, when relating the events of the trip, I forgot my role as spy. My voice would rise in excitement when I talked about riding in the Rolls Royce. Immediately, my mother's face darkened and her mouth became a grim line.

"Maybe you would like to live there with them. Maybe you should have just stayed out there and never come back."

"No! The Rolls Royce was stupid, but it was fun riding down Hollywood Boulevard. That's what was fun. Not being with them. Not being in a car with a gold thing on the hood. Not being stared at wherever we went. That wasn't fun at all."

She calmed down. Her shoulders relaxed. "As long as you didn't enjoy yourself."

"Oh no. I didn't. Not at all." I wouldn't mention Disneyland.

"Good. That's what's important."

I understood her concern. In the short time we were there, the things that had seemed so odd, things we'd laughed at behind our hands, had started to become normal. I already missed sitting down at a breakfast table with servants behind me, waiting to bring me blueberry pancakes or French toast with bananas if I asked for it. I already missed clean sheets that felt wonderful against my skin, and going barefoot through the house without getting my feet dirty. I already missed fluffy towels and the feeling that everything was in control and everything was being taken care of and everything in the world was okay. It was a place where the sun always shined through clean windows, and nothing broke, and nobody shrieked and threw hairbrushes. If it wasn't for the old lady, I might even understand why my father liked his life without us. We were dark and dirty; we were the broken glass in the sidewalk cracks. We were smudged windows and the wino on the street corner with the cardboard sign. And yes, we were thrift-shop clothes.

But sometimes I forgot that my father had made us this way. Poor, ragged, nasty brats. It was a good thing my mother was around to remind me.

Chapter 6

Florida, present day

The second morning of my visit to Florida I have two text messages, one from my son, one from my daughter. They both wish me happy birthday, and both ask how it's going. I'm lying on my back on the floor mattress, and I text my thanks and tell them I will try to call in the evening. After I send the messages, I listen for any sounds outside my door. The house is silent. Not a tick of a clock or the jingle of a dog collar. I recheck the time on my phone and confirm that it's eight-thirty. I slip into black shorts, black T-shirt, and flip-flops. My father's door is closed, and I move down the hall to the kitchen expecting to find him at the table. He's nowhere around, and I decide he's still in bed. Odd. Should I check on him? I imagine opening his bedroom door to find him dead. Happy birthday. Love, Dad.

I hear the sound of movement, and the click of a door latch. The dogs appear, giving me a hello, shooting through the doggy door to run in the backyard, reappearing next to me to beg for breakfast. Dad finally shows up and takes his seat at the table, waiting for the day to mysteriously unfold in front of him.

"Is there anything you'd like to do today?" I ask as I put a bowl of oatmeal in front of him.

"You know what?" He braces both arms on either side of his bowl and looks up at me. "I'd like to go shopping for a birthday gift." He smiles, proud of himself.

I'm shocked that he would remember my birthday. Since I never existed, my birthday never existed, and his out-of-character response, combined with the thought of his wanting to get me something at this moment in his life, makes me uncomfortable.

"Carol's birthday is today," he announces. "And I'd like to get her a gift and a card."

Everything makes sense now. Carol and I have discussed how odd it is that we have the same birthday. "What would you like to get her?" I ask.

"I don't know."

"What does she like?"

"I don't know."

I'm pretty sure his answer would have been the same regardless of his Alzheimer's. He likes to be around people, but he doesn't take an interest in the details of their lives. This is nothing new. "She's worked for you for years." I keep my voice light.

"I don't really know her."

"She likes plants," I tell him. "And wine. Maybe a plant and a bottle of wine?"

"And a card," he says. "We have to get a card."

Once we finish breakfast and the dogs are fed, we head out on the gift and card quest. I knew when I booked my flight that he wouldn't know today was my birthday, but I hadn't planned on his remembering someone else's birthday while forgetting mine.

"I'll drive," Dad says, walking toward his van.

My rental car is blocking the way. "Let's just take my car." I'm amazed that he's still driving, and I don't want to get in a car with him. I imagine ending up in a wreck where I become bedridden and unable to return home, trapped in the hot stuffy bedroom while my father takes care of me in a fashion that pays homage to Stephen King's *Misery*.

This whole endeavor, this trip to hell on my birthday, reeks of the masochism my mother's side of the family is so famous for, but in reality I spent a week trying to find a block of days that didn't contain my birthday. Impossible. Writers look at bad situations through a different lens, and my own dark humor allows me to hope that I'm about to embark upon the most bizarre birthday ever.

I don't know my way around town, and Dad only knows how to get to three places: Home Plate, church, and the fruit stand.

"Maybe this way." He points to the right. It's a busy road, so I take it.

"Maybe make a left at this light," he says after we've gone about four miles. I'm dropping mental breadcrumbs so I can find my way back.

"Oh, I don't know." He's confused and disgusted with himself.

"We'll go a little farther. I see some shops up ahead."

And there it is. A Publix grocery store. I park, and we go inside, Dad shuffling beside me. It's called the

Alzheimer's gait, and I slow to match his speed. "What are we doing here?" he asks.

"A birthday present for Carol."

"Oh, that's right." But I'm not sure if he really remembers, or if he's just playing along.

"There's the plant section." I point, and we do more shuffling.

Once there, we find some lovely and unusual mums. "This looks nice." I hold up a plant, and he agrees that it's a winner. Next comes a bottle of wine and a funny card, and we are checking out. Last time I visited, he lost his driver's license and credit card, so I watch to make sure the card is returned to his billfold rather than his shirt pocket.

Back home, we put the gifts on the counter and he sits down at the table to sign the card. Then he seals the envelope, writes Carol's name on the outside, and places it on the kitchen counter along with the plant and wine.

It's time for lunch, and he opens the refrigerator to see what he can find.

"There's an apple pie in here!" He's standing in front of the open door, his mouth agape, the pie at eye level. "Where did that come from? Did Carol bring it?"

I'm beginning to imagine how singers must feel when they've performed the same song thousand of times. There's nothing behind the words. "I made it yesterday." Before he can launch into a repeated conversation, I add, "Would you like a sandwich and a piece of pie?"

"That would be great." He checks the watch on his wrist that seems to be the only anchor he has to the passing of the day. "Later we'll go to church, then to Home Plate."

I can see I'm not going to get out of either. "What time do you usually leave for church?"

"Five o'clock." His mind jumps to what we will do once church is over. The things that haven't yet happened he seems able to conceptualize, but once they have occurred they are gone for good. "I hope you don't mind sitting at the bar," he says. "I like to sit at the bar. I always sit at the bar."

I used to tend bar, and I know the people who sit at the bar do so for company, to hang out with other patrons. "That's fine with me."

He eats the sandwich, then I put a slice of warm pie in front of him.

"Apple pie! Where did that come from?"

*

At five o'clock, we get in the rental car and head to church. This is a new place, and far from Dad's house. We pass several charming and beautiful churches on the way, navigate five miles of road construction to end up on a highway where cops are directing traffic the way they would for a football game. I turn in the drive, and men in orange vests that match the orange cones at their feet point us to the next available parking spot. Outside a building that looks like a theater complex, a screen is ticking down the minutes until the service begins. Inside is a concession counter where people are buying snacks.

"You aren't from around here."

I look up to see dad's neighbor coming our direction, a friendly smile on his face. I laugh at his comment, because it's the truth. I'm wearing a mod skirt with black sneakers and a black hoodie, and I'm sure the fluorescent light is bringing out the faded Manic Panic in my hair. But Ted is glad we're here, and we chat a bit, then move into the auditorium.

I've never been in a mega church, but I've seen them along the highways in Minnesota. It reminds me a bit of the Mall of America, and we sit down with the promise of sensory overload in our immediate future. Three massive viewing screens, a stage with flashing lights, three videographers at the back of the room, sitting on elevated platforms. People are eating snacks and drinking pop and coffee, and it feels a lot like a movie theater before the show begins.

I'm already creeped out.

Church is a relatively new thing for my father. It's something that started after he and Eve moved to Florida, and this church came recommended by Ted. My dad has talked about how friendly everyone is, but the friendliness is nothing but a Walmart greeter thing, people positioned at the various doors in order to welcome the congregation. There is very little recognition going on.

And then it starts. A band comes onstage and they tell us to stand. I'm used to loud music, I'm used to rock bands, but this is something beyond music, almost as if it's supposed to be a joke. I look around, but nobody is laughing. Many are holding their hands in the air, waving. Some couples cling to one another and sway with the music. Dad stands there, staring at the stage, his face expressionless as he takes in the window rattling, eardrum-shattering noise. Two guitars, bass, drum kit, mega amps. I want to leave, and I keep thinking the noise will soon stop. But it doesn't. And the clock on the screen keeps ticking.

Thirty minutes in, the band departs and we can finally sit down, and two men appear on stage with carryout coffee in their hands. They sit in overstuffed chairs and have what is supposed to be an impromptu chat, but it's heavily rehearsed and painful to watch, like a poor high school play. And then, thankfully, it's over and the band starts again. I can't take it anymore; I get up and leave. The service ends, and Dad joins me in the lobby a few minutes later.

We head to the bar. Dad was right when he said the bar was six or seven miles from his house. I'm driving, and he's giving me directions, and he's so on the ball that I almost forget he has dementia.

"At the next light, turn left and stay on the inside lane. A block past the light you'll make another left. The speed limit here is twenty." I'm not the greatest driver, and it's possible his driving would be better than mine.

The bar is located at one end of a small strip mall, a chalkboard easel listing the day's specials.

The place is packed, and the waitresses are dressed in black short-shorts and tight, low-cut T-shirts that reveal a lot of breast. Definitely a Hooter's rip-off. The room is deep and narrow, the two long walls lined with flats-screen televisions that are drowned out by blaring music. My dad pantomimes that we should work our way past the tables to the bar. I'm already feeling smothered, and people are staring at me. I'm sitting in the heart of conservative Florida, and I know I don't belong here.

Dad comes to this place seven nights a week. He's even returned the same night, forgetting that he'd been once already. That's how much he loves it. He thinks about it from the time he gets up until he goes to bed. And as we make our way through the crowd, people turn and greet him with a smile and a hello. He introduces me, but avoids using names. He can't remember them, and I wonder how long it would take for him to forget this place if he stopped coming. A week? Earlier, I'd asked him about his old favorite place, a place called Vickie's that he used to visit every evening, and he had no recollection of it. So maybe that's why he comes every night. If he doesn't, it will be gone. Erased.

At one time, he deliberately erased people from his memory, and now he spends his days clinging to what little memory he has left. And as he wades through the noise and crowd of faces that belong to names he can't recall, the darkness of what is now his life is something I can taste.

A young waitress with long, dark hair and a lot of makeup appears in front of him with a tray. "The bar is full," she says. "You'll have to sit at a table tonight." Se smiles sweetly, and tips her head in apology. "Sorry, hon."

"That's okay," he tells her.

"I won't be able to wait on you."

Her news is a blow to him, and his face falls.

She tells me her name is Octavia. "Your dad comes here every night."

I look at him, and he's already forgotten his disappointment. He's smiling, and his eyes are shining as he stares at Octavia with the lovesick crush of a smitten teenager.

And now it all makes sense. Why he didn't want to skip even a single night. Why he wanted to sit at the bar—her station. He comes here seven nights a week, more when he forgets he's already come, to see Octavia. It isn't the food, it isn't the other people; it's Octavia. And what's odd is that he has enough discretion to keep it a secret, to not admit that he has a crush on the waitress. Or does he even know? Is he consciously aware of his infatuation?

She could be a genuinely nice person, but at the same time I find myself thinking it's a good thing

Dad's will is locked up tight and the bulk of his estate left to his dead wife's kids and grandkids. Otherwise I feel pretty confident it would all go to Octavia. And yet, what difference would that make? If it did go to Octavia? I ponder the idea and find myself liking it.

These people, these strangers he faintly recognizes but can't fully recall, know he's messed up, know he can't remember them or anything that happened one minute ago, and I get the sense that they look out for him. And once again I feel the loss of a relationship he and I never had, and I know that this is the result of the choices he made. These people are his family, and he visits them every night for a few hours. At the same time I feel resentful that this is his life, yet I also feel guilty for not pulling him out of it. But this is what he wants. The noise and the smiling strangers. The deafening roar that evens the playing field, because nobody completely knows what's being said or what's going on. They lean forward, they say words that can't be heard, and they nod as if they understand.

It's happy hour, and as we sit at a table another waitress brings Dad a glass of red wine. He's nice to the young girl, but he can't help but look longingly through the crowd for a glimpse of Octavia. There are a few single seats at the bar, but no doubles. If I weren't here, he would have sat at the bar. He doesn't say this, but I know he's thinking it. And I imagine he's thinking that tomorrow he will come back, and when he does he will sit there, and Octavia will wait on him. And he will drink his wine and tell her stories she's heard a million times.

Is Florida filled with people like him? Lonely widows and widowers who have moved far from family and friends and now seek out the company of strangers?

A man and woman pause on their way to an empty table. The man puts a hand on Dad's shoulder. "Hello, Warren. We missed you last night!"

They're vaguely familiar to Dad, and he plays along, acting as if they're old friends. "This is my daughter," he tells them. He knows who I am tonight.

They're happy to meet me, but I can see the concern and confusion in their eyes. These are some of the people who look out for my father, and they wonder where I've been.

"We're really close," Dad tells them. He has the need to make others believe and see the path he wishes he'd taken. "My daughter and I have a great relationship."

I feel like a prop in this life he's fabricated for strangers. He would never say such words to me, and I think about how today is my birthday. I see his brain as a jumble of puzzle pieces he's constantly rearranging as he rewrites the past, turning it into something he can live with, removing regrets, mistakes, and selfish choices in order to suit his own desires and needs. In his broken mind, the things a stronger man would have done become the things he really did so that he can be the hero of his own story. But I'm the one he abandoned, and I know the truth.

Before excusing themselves, the couple and I exchange phone numbers and email addresses, and I'm sure I will get a report that will further explain the worry in their eyes.

Because we can't sit at the bar, we eat quickly and leave. The night is unfulfilled, but tomorrow will be better. It's still light when we get back to Dad's house, and the early return has him confused. He's ready to head for bed, but it's only a little after seven.

Carol stops to check on him as she probably does most evenings. She's in her mid-forties and attractive, wearing dress shorts, heels, and a clingy, low-cut top that shows off her figure. After the visit to the bar, I find myself wondering if Dad ever flirts with her. And now that she's here, I can't help but notice a change in their relationship. On my previous visits he talked about her nonstop, and when she arrived at his house he would light up. Now that response is reserved for Octavia.

Dad gives Carol the birthday presents.

"You know what I like," she says, admiring the mum with its bright orange flowers.

Dad nods happily. "I sure do."

She stays a few more minutes, then, with a laugh, says she's going home to drink the wine.

Once Carol is gone, my dad gives the dogs treats from a jar next to his chair, shuffles to the kitchen, opens the refrigerator, and marvels at the pie that has once again magically appeared. I head down the hallway to the bathroom— the only way to have a few moments alone.

While I'm in the bathroom, Dad shouts to me from the other side of the door.

"Hey, I want to ask you something!" He pauses to line up his question. "What about your mother?"

I don't want to come out, but I wash my hands and join him in the hall. A part of me wonders if there's any way my mother and father can have a relationship. Not as a couple, but as two people who share a past. And how long does he have left? How long before he forgets her as well as everyone else? Should I try to find her? Maybe take my laptop to a café and do a search? Is she still married? Is her husband still alive?

The last time I saw her she was standing over my hospital bed screaming and sobbing, but mostly screaming, all because my husband had called my father. Nurses appeared at the hospital room door, and she'd been asked to leave. Escorted out.

I have no desire to get in touch with her. To tell her of Dad's interest. But there is so little time left … If he didn't have Alzheimer's, would he have this obsession? Under normal circumstances, his fixation would lead me to believe he's never forgotten her and he's continued to think about her over the years. He was a secretive man, and does he now simply lack the discretion to keep those secrets, those thoughts, to himself? Has she been in his head for the past fifty years? Did he ever regret the choices he made?

He can no longer answer these questions.

In the back of my mind, I always thought there would come a time when he and I would get to know each other. Maybe after he retired, or once his wife was gone. *She lived so long.* That wouldn't happen now.

This person beside me isn't the person he once was. He almost seems a vault of random memories and random emotions, snapshots of external actions combined with new, mimicked behavior that has little connection to the person he used to be. He moves through the day, watching the clock, eating his meals, feeding the dogs, mowing the yard, going to the bar, but these actions seem to come from a place rooted in repetition.

Once he sits down in a quiet room, once his focus is removed from the chaos of the church and the chaos of the bar, from whatever task is at hand, his thoughts swing back and he remembers the beautiful woman with the dark hair and red lips, he recalls waking up with her on a sunny morning, he remembers a time when life was so much more than it is now, a time when he was adored and loved. He remembers a life he left behind.

What if he'd stayed?

I'm not sure he can form such an abstract thought, but he probably feels the shadow and shape of that unlived, unfinished life.

We would have been poor. We would have stayed in Florida. My mother would never have moved to New Mexico, never remarried. I would never have met my husband, or had the children I have now. I would have met someone else, some other man and we would have had children that I loved as much as my children. I don't like to think about such things, because I can't imagine a world without the two people I cherish the most, my son and daughter.

I don't like the turn my mind has taken tonight. Dad's rambling memories shine a dim light on the past, then shut off before I can fully grasp what I've seen. He moves on while I remain in the scene he presents to me.

Maybe the life he shared with my mother is now so vivid because it was his only real life. The life he shared with Eve was no more real than the life he has now. He'd become a part of it, fallen easily into a role because he wanted to experience a world he'd never known. But it hadn't been real, not down-to-earth real in the way his first marriage, his first and possibly only love, had been. He gave up love for material wealth. It's an old plot of many a morality tale, with a familiar ending: powerful, tragic, sad.

My father and I take our seats in the living room in front of the big-screen TV. He once again feeds the dogs treats, forgets he's just done it, and feeds them treats again, even though I try to stop him. Then he turns to me, elbows on his knees, his face earnest in the way of someone about to embark upon a great and never-before-shared conversation. It has taken a lot for him to gather the courage to launch this rare and formerly taboo topic.

"What do you hear from your mother?" More questions follow: How is she doing?" Where does she live? Is she still beautiful?" When he talks about her, he lights up, and a depth that wasn't there a moment ago replaces the flatness in his eyes. For a brief time, they're the eyes of someone who is still alive.

Chapter 7

"You should move here," my dad says.

It's the day after my birthday, and we're sitting at the breakfast table. I've just put a plate of eggs and toast in front of him, along with coffee, juice, and his morning medicine. I'm not sure if he's ever as much as poured himself a bowl of cereal, and now it's too late for him to learn the most basic of skills. Every morning he sits and waits for the food to come.

"I can't move to Ocala," I tell him.

"Why not? I have plenty of room. You can live with me."

There are some who wonder why I have anything to do with my father, and others, like Eve's sons, who think I should pack up and move to Florida to take care of him.

"I wouldn't want to be so far from my kids," I say.

"How far is it to your house?" he asks. He can't visualize me anywhere but standing right in front of him.

"About fifteen hundred miles."

"Oh!" He's shocked, a shock formerly reserved for the apple pie. "That's a long way!"

"Minnesota is way up there." It's best to explain things in short, simple sentences. "Almost to Canada."

That helps, and comprehension dawns. Minnesota is no longer this vague state in the Midwest. He has a place to put it.

"Maybe I could drive to see you," he says.

He's worried about being alone again, and I wonder if my visit was a bad idea. "It's too far for you to drive," I tell him. I try to imagine him heading from Florida to Minnesota. I doubt he'd even get out of town.

"I could bring the dogs," he says, as if the dogs are his only hurdle.

"You'd have to fly if you came to visit me. Carol could put you on a plane in Orlando, and I'll pick you up at the airport in St. Paul."

He used to restore antique planes, and up until a few years ago he had a private pilot's license, but he's never liked to fly commercial and I can see the idea of getting on a plane is unappealing to him.

"Where do you live?" he asks.

"Minnesota." Once again, I wonder if he knows who I am, wonder if he's dropped that thread and thinks I'm a stranger who's stopped by to check on him. It's hard to say. Most of the time I get the sense he sees me as two people, a stranger and his daughter.

"You should move here," he repeats, unwilling to let go of the idea. I hope it's not going to become a conversation we have twenty times today. "I have plenty of room. You can have the bedroom at the end of the hall."

He and I have come full circle, except that now he's the child and I'm the adult. This time, he's begging me to stay and I'll soon be the one walking out the door. The cruelty of my next thought shames me: *You reap what you sow.* My reaction is unfair, because this is no longer the man who walked away; this is someone else, an old, lost, lonely stranger. "I'll try to come back for another visit in a few months." In a couple of days, maybe less, he will forget I was here, while I won't be able to quit rerunning the events of the past few days, trying to sort out what can't be sorted out. How does Carol do it? The same conversations twenty times a day? Yet she doesn't have the emotional connections to the things he says. His words are just words, just tedious stories that might or might not be true, some being the things he wished he'd done.

"I don't know why you won't move here," he says.

"I can't."

"Why not?"

I try a different tactic. Something very basic that he might understand. "I don't like Ocala. I wouldn't want to live here."

He's stunned. "Eve loved it. She said it was the best place she'd ever lived. Why don't you like it?"

How do I go into the aesthetic qualities of a town? "Too much sprawl." But that's what Florida is all about. "And I don't like hot weather."

"I wish you would stay longer. I wish you wouldn't leave so soon. Can you leave later? What do you have waiting for you at home? Why do you have to get back? I really wish you'd move here."

We finish breakfast and head to the living room. We take our chairs, the recliner and the magic lift. For the next two hours, I listen to his stories. He is always the star, the hero, the main character. Sometimes he relates an event that he wasn't a part of, something he may have seen on the news, but in his revised version he's the center of the story, he's involved in the plot, maybe even driving it. This is about him. A world he's seeing in his mind, always told from his point of view. He's the old drunk guy at the end of the bar who never stops talking. He needs an audience. He needs to tell his stories.

I've come to realize that being around someone with Alzheimer's is like being around someone who's really, really wasted. And like someone who's had way too much too drink, his mood and attention swings from one subject and emotion to another.

Now he pauses, spots something else in his brain, then launches into another topic: "I've been a bad, bad person."

For once I can follow his train of thought as he tries to figure out why I'm unwilling to extend my stay or even move in with him for a while. He is somehow able to correlate my unwillingness to become deeply involved with him and his present situation to his absence in my life. And I find myself wondering if he actually feels guilt over what he's done, or is his current reaction a manifestation of his selfishness? Is he simply analyzing the cause and effect of his actions?

"Why do you say you're bad?" I ask. I know I should try to take his thoughts in a different direction, but I want to know if he's actually felt remorse all of these years.

"I abandoned you."

Such words coming from his mouth are totally foreign.

"I walked out and never looked back. I was an awful person. Awful."

He's always known what he did. This is the information delivered by his confession. *He's always known.*

In the past, whenever I tried to understand how a person could so thoroughly leave his family, I've always concluded that he didn't know the extent of his crime. He was young. He was foolish. He just didn't realize, or just didn't think about the impact his actions would have. And maybe he didn't even realize what he was doing was morally wrong.

But he knew. He *knew.*

I feel sick to my stomach. Moments ago, I worried about leaving him, but suddenly I feel the need to get away from this person who is telling me things he shouldn't tell me. Has he forgotten who I am again? How much longer until I can leave? I do a mental calculation. Forty-eight hours. How can I stand it? Knowing what I know? Do I have the strength for this?

Leave your wife and children, never have contact with them again, and I will give you a life of luxury.

He sold his soul. And he'd done it with both eyes open.

I'm surprised by my own shaky reaction, because I thought I'd moved past my father long ago. I didn't think he could ever hurt me again. I didn't think he could mess with my head. But he can. And the way he keeps talking about things I don't want to know and things I don't want to hear … I feel like the sin eater. I feel like he's dumping all of this on me, when he should be talking to a priest or minister. He wants me to pack up his mistakes and carry them away with me. Back home, I will line them up on the shelf and look at them every day. Bugs trapped in amber. That's how it feels. These things he's telling me that I don't want to know. I'm overreacting, but it suddenly seems so evil. His life. Yes, I knew his abandonment was all about status and materialism, but his new revelations cover it with a darkness that borders on evil. Or do I just want to make this all black and white so I can walk away? I want to walk away.

I see the shame in his eyes. A shame he's been able to keep buried until now. But Alzheimer's seems to have a way of unlocking the deepest secrets. He's lost the ability to control the thoughts he doesn't want to have, and now they come at him full-force, like a bucket of sins he's spent his life trying to forget, the memories of the bad things becoming stronger and impossible to hide.

Like all things in this claustrophobic world that belong to my father's mind, the horror I'm feeling comes edged with an odd sense of relief. I finally know he was fully aware of what he was doing, that his abandonment was a conscious choice rather than the actions of a man who hadn't stopped to think things through. The weird twist is that I've always felt bad because I stopped loving him years ago. Once love is killed so thoroughly, it can't come back. Right now I feel a sense of affection and certainly a sense of responsibility for the man in the chair across the room, but not love. And his confession makes the lack of love easier to accept. I try to tell myself that now, knowing what I finally know, I can embrace the lack of love without guilt. I'm the one who could fix this, who could take that mental step, but I don't need to. I don't have to. It's okay to not love my father.

But that acknowledgement makes me incredibly sad, and I think about what could have been, what should have been. I want to tell fathers how important they are, and I want to tell them to call and write and remember their children. Because after a while, the door closes on a child's heart and it can't be reopened.

Chapter 8

The Man Who Stayed

New Mexico, late sixties

I slipped the 45-RPM record on the metal spindle and followed with the plastic arm to hold it in place. The player was one of those portable things, a cube with a latch on one side and a cloth-covered speaker in front. It smelled good. Like cardboard and fabric and hot, dusty wires.

My mother and David were getting married in two hours, and I was in my bedroom wearing a new dress, waiting to head to church.

How we ended up in New Mexico was just another bad decision in a string of bad decisions. My mother followed a man from Iowa to Albuquerque. Once there, she discovered he was married. With no money to return to Iowa, we were stuck. But Albuquerque was a minefield of new men, and they began showing up, one crazy loser after the other. Until she met David …

I'd never heard of a Christian Brother until David had come along, but apparently they were like priests except they couldn't say mass. And like priests, they couldn't get married and they couldn't have kids.

"I'm his first and only girlfriend," my mother had told me. "Forty years old, and he'd never even kissed a woman."

He may have left the Christian Brothers, but he was still a Catholic and couldn't marry my mother since she'd been married once before. This had been good news to me, and I'd breathed a huge sigh of relief when I'd heard it. David would go away; he would move on like the rest of them. But David knew people. People who apparently had connections upstairs, and in a short amount of time my mother was no longer a divorcee.

"My marriage to your father has been annulled," she told me one day at our little house in Albuquerque.

"So the Church is saying you've never been married?" I thought about the wedding album, wondering what she'd do with it. And the wedding dress. What about the wedding dress?

"That's right."

I could see that she loved the idea of her first marriage not counting. My dad may have walked out on her, but in her mind a man couldn't really leave a woman if they'd never been married in the first place. David was not only her do-over, he would be her first husband. Was the annulment about marrying David or about erasing my father in an even bigger way than he'd erased us? Hadn't she and I laughed together about David just a week ago? Hadn't we made fun of him behind his back?

"But you have kids," I said. "What about Dad? What about us? Does that mean he was never our father?" It was too much for me to grasp, and I don't know what upset me more, knowing she would be able to marry this odd new man, or finding out I was a bastard and had never had a father. I didn't like any of it.

"David has always dreamed of being married and having a family. Now he has one. He'll be your father."

Over the past six years, she'd brought a lot of creepy men into our lives. Now one of those men was going to be a permanent fixture. "He will never be my father." I wanted to get that straight.

"I've already talked to Jude, and he wants to be adopted. David will adopt both of you. You'll finally have a father. A real father."

"No." I wanted to say that the weirdo would never be my father, but I restrained myself. She must like him. At least a little. I couldn't talk bad about him. But couldn't she see how wrong he was? Why was she doing this?

"You and Dad were married. How can you suddenly say you weren't? Weren't you married in a church? By a priest? I don't get it."

"Sometimes the Church can decide that a marriage wasn't a real marriage even if everything was legal. The first marriage was not a real marriage in the eyes of God."

"That seems dishonest to me. You were married. It was real." What she was saying is that they'd found some religious crook to fill out some paperwork claiming her first marriage wasn't a real bond so that David could feel okay about marrying a divorced woman. The first marriage *was* real. They couldn't change that with a piece of paper signed by a couple of cardinals.

"I'm sure there are other men you could marry," I'd said. "What about Ralph? I like Ralph."

Ralph was an artist, and he'd adored my mother. He wouldn't have insisted upon an annulment. "Or the guy with the horses. What about the guy with the horses?" Anybody seemed better than the dork with the pocket protector, clip-on ties, clip-on sunglasses, coin purse, billfold-dental pick, poached-egg maker, protractor, Polaroid camera, galoshes, plaid shirts, beige pants, bicycle with saddle bags, metal lunch box and metal thermos, shoe horn, and shoe polish, who'd never kissed a girl until he'd met my mother.

"David and I are getting married, and you'll just have to accept it," she'd said.

Was everything just moving too quickly? Had she gotten herself into something she didn't know how to get out of? "But you made fun of him," I reminded her.

Her girl-talk face, the one she'd worn when she told me about menstrual periods and the rhythm method, vanished, and she glared at me with a hatred I'd come to recognize. "I don't want you to ever say that again," she said. "Ever."

Right then and there I understood that this was a new world. There would be no more shared jokes, especially shared jokes about David. The fragile and weak mother/daughter bond died that day.

The courtship had been short, and my brother and I hadn't gotten to know David. My mother deliberately kept us apart, and the two of them spent weekends together while Jude and I stayed with friends. David was just a stranger I hoped would eventually go away like the rest of them. Instead, he asked my mother to marry him, and she said yes.

The marriage meant this was our life. There would be no more new adventures, no more creeps, no chance that this life would soon be traded for another.

The walls of our small Albuquerque house were made of cement block, the ceilings were low, and the roof was flat. Tiny kitchen, tiny bathroom, two tiny bedrooms, with an attached garage that had been converted into a third bedroom. I used the garage on days like today, when the weather wasn't too hot or too cold, and at age fourteen it was nice to have a space of my own.

Right now, the house was full of people. I could feel them beyond my door, and I could hear voices and footsteps, and water running in the kitchen sink, and the sound of silverware and glasses and plates.

Preparations to leave. Relatives from Iowa and friends from Albuquerque were here.

Three years earlier, my mother had gotten a job as a secretary at the Veteran's Administration, and she'd been able to buy the house and a new car. We didn't have much money for clothes or food, but we didn't go to school hungry anymore. I was proud of her.

My mother had grown up. There was very little sobbing and very little hairbrush throwing. The turning point had come with a woman named Stella. Stella brought common sense and fun into our lives. She was a good person. A kind person. And I think she was in love with my mother.

I liked to imagine our life as a graph, and everything below the centerline was bad, everything above it was good. Stella had taken us to the top of the page and kept us there.

And then David showed up, a blind date, arranged by a co-worker, taking place when my mother was feeling okay about being a single woman with two kids. It would have been three kids if Thomas had come back, but no amount of begging could convince him to leave Iowa, where he'd been sent to live with our grandmother. I didn't blame him.

Before David, my mother had been happy. And not momentarily happy. I knew what that looked like. She'd been happy for two years.

If David had come earlier, I might have understood my mother marrying him. But now, when her life seemed about perfect ... I didn't get it. I didn't get it at all. She was less when she was with him. She wasn't herself when she was with him.

Maybe the marriage would work, I'd told myself when it became apparent that nothing was going to change my mother's mind. Maybe it would be okay. And if it didn't work, we would move on. Marriage seemed to just be a piece of paper anyway. This marriage could be annulled like the first one.

I pushed the cream-colored lever to *Auto*. The player clicked, then the record dropped and the needle arm lifted, moved into position, and lowered to the spinning vinyl. A few cracks and pops and the song began.

"Going to the Chapel," by the Dixie Cups. I'd been saving it for this moment, just minutes before we left for the church. Everybody would get a kick out of it.

There had been a somber tone to the gathering of people. Not excitement, but a nervousness. I wasn't the only one who thought the marriage was a bad idea. Everybody seemed to disapprove, especially David's family, and Stella had even attempted to talk my mother out of it. That conversation had created a tension between the two women that hadn't eased.

The pop song changed the mood of the house. The noise level increased. Relatives poked their heads inside the bedroom to laugh and show their appreciation of my music choice.

I heard a flurry of movement in the hallway. Rapid footsteps. And then my mother was there, in the doorway, carried in on the laughter of friends and relatives. She kept a smile on her face until the door closed behind her. Then she came at me, teeth gritted. "Shut that off!"

Stunned, I lifted the needle from the record, plunging the room into silence. "I thought you'd like it," I said. "I thought it was funny."

She was crying now, and her makeup was running. We were supposed to leave for church in a few minutes. I hadn't seen her this upset in a long time. Up until now, there had only been one person who could cause this level of hysteria: my father.

I'd been proud of my little plan to make people laugh, to loosen everybody up.

"You horrible, horrible thing." She whispered so no one beyond the bedroom would hear. She was dressed in a white suit with a pastel corsage. Her dark hair had been ratted high on top, with two curls on each cheek. Her lipstick was perfect.

I grabbed a handful of tissue and threw it at her.

At first she didn't understand, but she finally made the connection and wiped her eyes. "You had to ruin this, didn't you?" She checked the tissue for black mascara.

"What are you talking about?" She may have thought I was mocking her, but I wasn't. That hadn't been my intention.

"I don't want to see your face the rest of the day, do you hear? Stay away from me. Just stay away!"

"How am I going to get to the church?" We'd planned to ride together.

"Find somebody else to go with. You are not getting in a car with me. You know what? Don't come. Don't bother coming at all."

She left, slamming the door behind her. I heard the drone of conversation, and my mother saying something about my cat and her allergies. Then she laughed.

The door opened and my uncle poked his head inside. "Everything okay in here?"

I nodded.

He stood there a moment as if he wanted to say something else, then he closed the door and left me alone. He knew how my mother could be.

Once my brain began working again, I realized what had happened wasn't about the music or about me. It was about the wedding. About David.

She didn't want to marry him.

Why couldn't she see that? Today wasn't a day for bubbly music or laughter. It was a funeral. I should have played "Abide With Me," or "End of the Road."

She was a woman in her late thirties who didn't understand her own heart and her own desires. But did anybody really know what they wanted? Would I know when I met the guy I wanted to marry? I liked the idea of arranged marriages. They made more sense than silly dating and lying and two people pretending to be who they weren't so they could marry each other.

When she put on the white suit, had she been thinking of another day, another wedding, another man? Church papers now said her first marriage had never taken place, but signatures couldn't undo the past. Today was supposed make her forget about her marriage to my dad. Instead, it brought it back. Was she thinking about the charming man who'd winked to someone beyond the edge of a photo album? A day when she'd been younger and prettier and had never thought her happiness would end.

Eight years since my father had left. Time didn't heal all wounds. I think time tricked people into thinking they were okay.

What if I didn't go to the wedding? What if I just stayed home?

I would be in so much trouble. There were things my mother told me to do that she didn't really mean. Things that, if I followed her instructions, would land me in a lot of trouble. No, I had to go.

I caught a ride with my best friend Robin and her mother, and I sat with them in church, far away from the family, toward the back. My friend's mother had once commented on the odd pairing, and almost everyone in the big Catholic church, except for David's family, had laughed and called him an oddball. Now those people sat in silence and would forever hold their peace, trying to forget that they'd made fun of my mother's new husband.

It was like watching strangers get married. They were too far away for us to hear what was being said, just the low murmur of voices. I wondered if her mascara was still smeared. I wondered if her eyes were still red.

Allergies.

Pretty soon it was over. Pretty soon the couple turned to the crowd, my mother with a white bouquet in her hands, a frozen smile on her lips. David's smile might have been more genuine, because, after all, he was getting what he wanted. A wife.

Everything for me was a blur. A reception was held in a VFW hall, I didn't know the location, something put together by David's sister. I wished I'd stayed home. My mother was too busy to have noticed my absence.

At some point, they'd changed clothes. She now wore a pantsuit. I remembered when she bought it— the going-away outfit, she'd called it.

Rice was thrown and the bouquet was tossed. A child from David's family caught it, a little girl in a long dress. I'd seen her earlier when the brat stuck out her tongue at me.

The pair got into my mother's blue Chevy Malibu. Someone—maybe one of David's nephews—had written *just married* on the back window. Tin cans rattled as the car pulled away. Nothing had ever felt so wrong, so forced, so unnatural.

Beyond the soaped window were the silhouettes of two heads; she sat in the middle. I tried to imagine what they would talk about on their way to the Grand Canyon. Would she cry? Would he not understand? Would his very ignorance make her cry more?

Stella appeared at my elbow. She was staying with my brother and me until my mother and David returned.

"There goes an odd couple," I said.

As soon as the car was out of sight, Stella crumpled. "I've lost my best friend." Tears ran down her cheeks. Stella was smaller than me, but tough. I'd never seen her cry, and I gave her shoulder an awkward pat. Poor Stella. My mother, baby brother, and I had spent almost every weekend and weeknight with her for the past two years.

"She's in love with you," I'd once told my mother.

"Well, I care about her, too. We're best friends."

"No, I mean she *loves* you."

"What are you talking about?" Her eyes flashed in anger.

"Never mind."

But Stella had been the driving force behind the change in my mother. She'd been the driving force behind my mother's contentment and happiness, and I would have been okay with Stella joining our family. I liked her. Had my mother never really known? I found that hard to believe, and yet she was naïve in a lot of ways. And lesbians weren't really talked about, not where we came from.

One thing I did know: Stella had been good for my mother. Stella had made my mother a better person. Stella had made us a family again. She'd been there for us in so many ways. We'd spent almost all of our free time with her, and when I visited my grandmother in the summer, Stella wrote to me. When I talked about getting my driver's license, Stella told me she would teach me how to drive, and she might even give me her gold Camaro when it came time to get a new vehicle. She was almost a parent to me.

But her grief over the wedding, the way she'd held it together until the moment the car turned the corner, surprised and shocked me.

"Why?" I asked, still staring at the place the car · had been, imagining the odd couple inside. It didn't make sense.

Stella shook her head. "I've been trying to figure that out." She pulled in a deep breath and straightened her spine. "I almost didn't come, "she confessed. "I didn't want to come. I didn't want to see it." But she'd done it for my mother. Just like she'd given her the Rodin statue, The Kiss, as a wedding gift. *It's okay. I'm okay with this. I'm okay with your having sex with a man, marrying a man.* But she wasn't. Maybe that's really what love was about. Stepping out of the way. Supporting the person you loved.

All this religion messed things up. David wanted to experience sex, and he couldn't have sex unless he was married. I didn't want to think about the two of them together in such an intimate way, but that's what it boiled down to. Those two people in the car, driving off to have sex.

"He wishes I could be a virgin," my mother had confided. "But he understands. He loves me anyway."

All this sex and marriage, male and female. The whole thing was so confusing. If only Stella could have been my second mother. I didn't think a person could just decide to be a lesbian, but weren't women better companions anyway? Stella was one of the few positive relationships my mother had ever had, male or female.

"I almost didn't come either," I told Stella.

"It won't be the same," she said. "Nothing will ever be the same."

Our life with Stella was over. When the honeymoon couple returned, we would move to southern New Mexico where David taught school, and Stella would no longer be a part of our lives. She would erase us, but it was an erasure I would understand.

People. What was wrong with them?

It seemed to me that every single drop of happiness or misery was the direct result of someone else. Why couldn't we be happy without other people? I didn't mean living on an island somewhere, but why did it take another person to make us happy or miserable? It wasn't right. I needed to figure out how to protect myself. I needed to think about this.

I gave Stella a hug. I would miss her terribly.

Chapter 9

Next to me in the backseat of the blue Chevy Malibu—windows cracked, wind whistling in—my younger brother, now six, jabbered and laughed while flipping through the pages of *MAD Magazine*. He was excited about starting a new life, excited about the strange man behind the wheel. But then my brother had never had a father. Maybe he was more excited about the idea of having a dad, not really thinking about who that dad would be. He seemed oblivious to the darkness of the situation and how incredibly wrong it felt.

We were one hundred and fifty miles south of Albuquerque, heading toward Roswell and coming out of a ninety-mile stretch of isolated desert highway, where we hadn't spotted a town, a gas station, or a single house.

Right now my mother was sitting in the middle of the front seat. Were they holding hands? They were. Ick.

I guess it made sense since they'd just gotten married, just gotten back from their honeymoon, but it was something I didn't want to witness or even think about. I'd rather they did that kind of thing in the dark, in the privacy of their bedroom.

In a short amount of time we would arrive in the little town of Artesia, where David taught college math. This meant I would once again start a new school in the middle of the year. People would stare, and I would keep my head down to avoid their bold eyes. I'd done this enough to know that there was always that one desperate, friendless person who attached herself to each new student until you shook her off.

David looked at me in the rearview mirror. "I've arranged for you to meet some children your age. I asked around at church, got some names, and one of the members offered the use of her house for a little party," he informed me. "She has two teenage boys."

"Um, no thanks." The last thing I needed was for David to find friends for me.

"It's already been scheduled," he said.

I glanced at my brother, looking for support. He seemed happy about the idea, but he'd been happy about the marriage, so what did he know? "I really don't want to go to any party," I said, trying to not freak out. "I'm sure I'll meet new people at school."

"The invitations have already been mailed." David leaned over, opened the glove box, and produced an envelope that he passed to the backseat.

I lifted the unsealed flap and pulled out a card. An invitation, with address and time. "A dance party?" What the hell?

"Keep reading." He leaned back, his seat pressing against my knees.

Come learn popular dance moves
taught by the newest teenager in town,
Theresa Balls.

I didn't know what made me madder, the part about the dance moves, or the use of David's last name. And it wasn't like I was some kind of dancer. I'd never taken any classes, but for some reason I could learn new dance steps in a short amount of time. Yes, I was good. Boys who ignored me during class lined up to dance with me at school events with live bands. My grandmother liked to say I could really cut a rug. But dancing, just letting the music carry you away, that was different. One time my mother invited a bunch of friends over with the idea that I would teach them all to dance. I tried, but I'd never seen so many people with no sense of rhythm, my mother being the worst of the lot.

I tossed the envelope and card to the front seat. "Are you kidding me?" Up until that point I'd tried to control my mouth. "There's no way I'm going to that. And my last name is not Balls." It was bad enough for him to use his name without asking me, but Balls? Balls? What kind of last name was Balls? I mean, that was the kind of name a person would have legally changed. You didn't keep that kind of name. That was as bad as saying your name was Mr. Shit.

"I thought you'd like to meet other kids your age." David glanced at my mother, worried that he'd already failed her. "The party is tomorrow." He was struggling with his new parental role. *How do I proceed? Do I insist she go, or back off?* "I suppose we could cancel. Or maybe just tell them you can't make it …" His words trailed off.

I crossed my arms and dropped back in my seat. I'd been cutting him too much slack, that's for sure.

I'd been too nice, too tolerant. "I don't know what you'll do, but I'm not going."

My little brother looked up from his *MAD Magazine* and inhaled. "I smell Artesia!"

Jude's job was to relieve tension, and he took that job seriously. All four of us laughed, and at least we could agree that my baby brother was adorable.

Chapter 10

Even though we were miles from town, Jude was right: we could smell our new home. Artesia made a person think of water, but Artesia's biggest export was oil from the refinery at the end of Main Street. My eyes and throat already burned, and I'd probably wake up with a headache tomorrow.

Before heading to our house, we hit the highlights and I quickly learned that Artesia was flat and colorless, like some faded Polaroid tucked away in a drawer. No trees, no grass, ugly buildings that made me feel uneasy if I looked at them too long. From the backseat, my eyes searched for some speck of beauty, a tiny bit of color, a blade of grass, a flower. The sky was the only thing that held any promise. It was vast, bigger than any sky I'd ever seen.

The town had a lot of drive-through liquor stores and drive-in restaurants and a drive-in theater on the edge of town, south of the oil refinery. Everything was old and faded and falling apart, as if the place had been worn down by a wind that never stopped blowing. Artesia felt like a sad movie, something in black & white about a poor rancher and the woman he loved who didn't love him back.   The rancher would drive into town in his battered truck, and she would serve him a meal at a little corner diner, and he would always leave a nice tip. This would continue through the years. While she refilled his white coffee mug, she told him about her marriage and about her children, and the rancher watched her grow old, never speaking of his love. That's how Artesia felt.

There were two grocery stores, a few restaurants, and the A&W where all the kids hung out. Everything seemed washed in a bleakness I couldn't quite put my finger on, something I didn't understand.

This was a place where kids "dragged the strip", and life appeared to take place in cars. Maybe the constant movement gave people the feeling that they were getting away, they were outrunning the town, tires moving restlessly over concrete streets with faded center lines and street lights that changed from red to green long after everyone went to bed.

Our tour included the College of Artesia located on the north edge of town. The buildings were surrounded by student housing, some of the dorms several stories tall, fighting the landscape, visual proof that you couldn't change the feel of a town by putting up buildings you might see in a city. They looked wrong and weird, and made me feel ever more uncomfortable than the structures that had stood a hundred years.

The whole place felt unfinished, unplanned, thrown-together, like aliens had beamed the college down from a little slice in the sky. The classrooms were the kind of buildings that could be moved from location to location. It didn't look like a college, but more like a construction site. Back in Albuquerque, Robin's mother had told me that it was a pretend school, a place for rich kids to dodge the draft. As proof, the parking lot was filled with shiny sports cars, and the few students I saw were clean-cut, not the typical hippies I was used to seeing near the University of New Mexico.

"These are just temporary buildings," David said, explaining his ugly classroom as he showed us around. A chalkboard, rows of desks.

Stepping through the doorway, we were immediately outside, standing in dirt and the glaring sun. From off in the distance came the echo of laughter and hollow music from small speakers. On the other side of a chain-link fence, bleach-blond girls with deep tans strolled around a swimming pool in tiny bikinis, while guys in swimming trunks lay on lounge chairs.

Even from such a distance, I could sense their privilege. Instantly, I knew they belonged to my dad's world.

*

In the heart of town, we turned down a residential street and pulled to a stop in front of a tiny, cement-block house with an attached garage and a yard of dirt and weeds.

"I can't wait to plant some grass and start mowing," David said.

That's what being married meant to him. Having a yard to mow on Saturdays. He may have lacked imagination, but he could dream of himself walking behind a lawnmower, a smile on his face. Just a regular married man.

Back in Albuquerque, my mother and David had talked about the projects they'd completed like painting and hanging curtains, but this would be my first glimpse of the new house. Each bedroom apparently had a color scheme, with custom curtains that would subtly reflect that color. My color was lavender, and my brother's was green. I understood that this was to make us feel special. But I think the curtains were like the lawn mowing, something that said this is official, this is real, as if custom curtains could somehow make us a family.

Inside, the house didn't get any less depressing, even though the cement-block walls had been given a fresh coat of white paint. The front door opened to a living room/kitchen combination, and the floor was green linoleum tile. Kitchen cupboards were of varnished plywood that had turned an ugly shade of orange.

"We're going to sand and paint those," my mother said.

"Avocado green," David added, watching her, waiting for her to approve his words.

"*Antique* avocado," she corrected.

"Antique."

This sounded like a project I wanted nothing to do with.

David excused himself to use the bathroom. As soon as he was out of earshot, my mother spun around and jabbed a finger into my chest. "You are going to that dance, do you hear me?" she said, her voice low, coming at me through gritted teeth. "And you are going to teach those kids the newest dance steps."

"Nobody even bothered to ask me. And did you see the name? That's not my name."

"You *are* going." Her fingers turned into a claw, and she grabbed me by the arm and pinched as hard as she could. I would have bruises tomorrow. Her next words were spit out one at a time. "Don't you dare ruin this for me." She'd held and hidden her anger for over an hour.

My little brother laughed, entertained by the scene and probably by the absurd idea of my teaching other kids to dance. Nobody was on my side.

A toilet flushed, a knob rattled, and a door opened. "Do you want to see your rooms?" David asked.

The hand on my arm dropped, and my mother turned toward the kitchen so her new husband couldn't see her enraged face.

David was tall—over six feet—and the ceiling seemed to almost touch his head. He had light-brown hair and thick glasses, and cheeks that were sunken. He *looked* like a math teacher. He kind of gave me the creeps, but I felt sorry for him at the same time. Maybe because he was like someone who'd spent the past thirty years in a state of suspended animation. He was a toddler in a man's body. I knew more about life than David did.

But then people said I was an old soul. At age fourteen, I considered myself somewhat of a philosopher, a student of human nature. I'd learned to read people by expression and gesture and tone of voice. In Albuquerque, classmates had come to me for advice. About boyfriends and girlfriends, school, parents. And I doled out wisdom like some reincarnated sage. It was too bad my mother hadn't asked for advice. I would have told her to run.

Even with three bedrooms, the house was tiny. We squeezed down a narrow hall with four doors, three opening to bedrooms, one to the only bathroom that was just as tiny as everything else. My bedroom was on the right at the end of the hall; my mother and her new husband's on the left. A person could stand and touch both doors at the same time. It was smaller than the tiny house we'd left in Albuquerque.

David waited for our response, hands folded, a proud expression on his face. I thought of all the places we'd lived, so many I'd lost count. This was David's first house. He was forty years old and he'd spent most of his life in isolation. He thought this building was wonderful. He thought his life with us and with my mother would be wonderful.

Yes, he irritated me, yes he had no business planning parties or giving me his name or telling me what to do, and yes I made fun of him behind his back, but the sympathy I felt in that moment was overwhelming. He was so naïve, so innocent. Something else prodded at the back of my brain, and it was the biggest reason I felt so incredibly sorry for this new man: I was pretty sure my mother didn't love him.

Chapter 11

"Your mother and I have come to a decision about your punishment," David said.

Sitting across from my brother, I poured milk on my Cheerios. "Punishment for what?" It was the day after we'd arrived in Artesia, and I'd just gotten up and wasn't yet wide-awake.

"For talking back to me," David said. "Your behavior and lack of respect is unacceptable." He wore jeans and a striped dress shirt; my brother and I were still in pajamas.

David unbuckled and removed his belt. "Your mother and I agreed on five lashes, plus the revocation of all privileges. You will be grounded for a month, starting today. You can eat meals with us, but after each meal you are to go directly to your room. You will also be expected to clean the house on Saturdays. Dust, vacuum, and scrub the bathroom."

I laughed.

This was like a bad school play, and he was a bad actor, his delivery stiff, with no genuine emotion behind it. "You're kidding, right?"

My mother emerged from the hallway. "Now it's ten!" She'd overheard our conversation.

She was a big finger-shaker, and her digit was in action. Shaking, pointing for added emphasis. "And today you will go to the dance party." Point, point. "You will stay in your room until this afternoon. David will take you to the party, and once you're home you'll go straight back to your room." She pointed down the hall. "Do you understand?" Pointed at me.

"This is crazy." I was the one who kept things going smoothly. I was the one who'd always held everything together. They were like two children reprimanding an adult.

"You've had no discipline in your life," David said. "But that is going to change today. From now on you will only speak when spoken to, and you will address me as Father or sir. Your mother has done a remarkable job, but you need a firm hand. You need strict rules and discipline. You need to learn manners and need to learn the proper way to treat adults. Do you understand?"

I glared at him.

"Do you understand?" he repeated, louder this time.

My younger brother sat at the table, silently watching while eating his cereal, making mental notes on how to behave and how to avoid just such a confrontation.

"Yeah." I used my eyes to tell David how much I despised him. *Read this.* I mentally threw him the finger.

"Yes, what?"

"Yes, sir."

David grasped the belt in both hands, displaying it in all its glory. Brown leather, about one and a half inches wide with a square gold buckle. I thought about stories I'd read like Oliver Twist and fairytales like Cinderella. They'd always seemed melodramatic, exaggerated. Strangers wouldn't come into a kid's life and suddenly start treating her in a horrible way. I mean, nobody would do that. But the evil stepmother and stepfather were real. And there was nothing at all interesting and unique about that discovery. This very scene had played out in houses across the country in one form or another. The weird thing is that David thought he was making the right decision. That's what I didn't get.

"Go to your room, put your hands on the bed, and bend over. I'll be there in a minute."

I laughed again. I couldn't help it. He was showing off. Showing off to my mother. And not doing a very good job of it as far as I was concerned.

"Go!" my mother screamed. And pointed.

"Are you really going to allow this stranger to … *spank* me?"

"Fifteen!" she shouted. "You will treat him with respect!"

I was pretty good when it came to figuring people out, understanding why they did what they did. But I was at a loss here. This was a moment I needed to freeze so I could examine it, because at the moment I could find no shred of reason behind their actions. I wanted to speak up for myself, tell him that he needed to respect *me*, but I was sure that would get me another five or ten lashes.

I shoved myself away from the table and strode down the hall to the bedroom. Fuming. I placed my hands on the mattress and leaned over. "I'm ready!" I shouted over my shoulder, doubting he would notice the hatred and sarcasm in my voice.

David appeared in the doorway, his face blank. He hadn't combed his hair, and a lock fell over his forehead. Seeing his blank face below his messy hair made me want to laugh again, and I willed my face to become as unemotional as his.

I wore thin cotton pajamas—matching top and shorts, pink with black cats. I wished I'd had time to get dressed. From now on I would put on jeans as soon as I woke up.

David entered the room and braced himself behind me, his body language saying he was doing something important, he was taking on the important role of father and head of the household. This was a part of his fantasy, just like the lawn mowing. This was his initiation into what he thought of as real life. This is what it meant to be married, what it meant to be a father and have a wife and family. He was playing house, and now it was time to spank the kid.

I heard movement, and saw my mother in the doorway, behind her, my brother. Their faces held expectation. Curiosity. And oddly, something I read as enjoyment.

The belt came down, and I turned away so none of them would see me wince. I refused to react. The blows hit my bottom and the tops of my legs. My mother was famous for her hairbrush throwing, and she sometimes struck us with wooden spoons, but those occasions had always been emotionally driven and somehow that had made them okay. She'd been out of control. Nothing like this. Not this planned persecution, this humiliation viewed by the whole family.

The moment was an important milestone for David, and I wanted to tell him he was a weak sissy. But that would be stupid.

"Harder," my mother instructed, as if she'd read my mind. She knew me too well. "You aren't hitting her hard enough."

It was like the marriage had sent her over the edge. That seemed the only logical explanation. She never thought she would marry David. It was all about getting my father's attention, one final attempt—a big one—to get him back. But he hadn't played right. He wasn't supposed to sign the annulment papers. He was supposed to beg her not to marry someone else. Maybe this had all been a ploy to shake him up, wake him up. Maybe he was supposed to have realized he would lose her for good if he didn't profess his love and admit to the mistake he'd made.

But he'd done none of the things she'd maybe hoped he would do, and now she was stuck in this nightmare. And she'd taken us with her.

The intensity of the blows increased as David counted. The math teacher. I wondered if my dad would care that some strange man was beating his daughter. Probably not. But he would never have spanked me. Ever. This I knew to be true.

David smelled like an old woman's house and clothes that had been put away sweaty, then worn again. And disturbingly, he smelled like my mother and her bath oil. I'd been told you could spray two fighting cats with the same perfume and they would get confused, think they were littermates. My mother had rubbed her scent on David, and he'd rubbed his scent on her, and now they were almost one person.

There were no words to convey how creepy the spanking was. It was more than discipline. Maybe later I would figure it out. No. I would push it from my mind. Forget it had happened. I was sensing a sort of warped perversion that was unlike anything I'd ever experienced. You know when something is wrong. When something isn't right.

I never made a sound. I wouldn't give any of them the satisfaction. When he was done, I straightened and looked him in the eye with a level of loathing that was entirely new to me.

I would have been nice to him. I would have been his friend even though he was a dork. Not now. I didn't say a word, but I hoped he would read my face, read my thoughts, and see how much I despised him and would always despise him.

"The party is at two o'clock," David said. "Be ready to go by one-thirty. And don't wear jeans and don't wear a miniskirt or mini dress. The nice girls around here don't wear those kinds of things."

Meaning I wasn't a nice girl.

"Wear the new dress. The one your mother bought for the wedding." He left, closing the door tightly behind him.

I did a mental calculation. How long until I could move out, how long until I reached eighteen? Four years.

I couldn't take this for four years.

I sat down gingerly on the bed. Ying, my Siamese cat, came out of hiding and joined me. I picked him up and hugged him to me, burying my face in his fur. Or could I leave at sixteen? I'd heard of kids leaving their families at sixteen. It was called emancipation or something like that. But I think they had to have a guardian, someone to maybe sign some papers. Could I take it for two years? My mind jumped. No way the marriage would last two years. My mother couldn't possibly stay with this guy that long. Maybe a year, tops. I could stand it for a year. And after that it would be the three of us again. We would laugh about the whole awful situation; we might even laugh about the look on David's face as he'd whipped me with the belt. So serious. So important.

I'm a married man now.

My mother had done not-so-smart things before, but she always snapped out of it. She would snap out of it again. For now I had to avoid looking either of them in the eye and avoid speaking to them. Keep my mouth shut and my head down, try not to draw attention to myself. One of these days it would all be over.

Thomas was lucky. By being bad he'd avoided this awfulness and was able to live someplace nice where nobody beat him. Thomas had almost choked me to death once, and I was sure he would beat David up if the man ever tried to spank him. Maybe he would kill him. I liked that idea. David dead. It would solve a lot of problems.

I heard a scraping noise followed by the appearance of a white paper plate under the door. Bare feet ran away. I put the cat aside and picked up the plate. In red crayon it read: PUT IN PANTS. I laughed. Yes, my brother was adorable.

*

The dress David told me to wear was the color of oatmeal and made of stiff, puckered fabric. Not seersucker, but something like it, only with bigger indentations. The cuffs and round neckline were trimmed with pink velvet ribbon. I'd never owned or worn anything like it, and I felt like a doll, kind of stupid but kind of nice at the same time. I added white fishnet stockings. On my feet I wore mod black ankle boots. My dark hair was parted in the center, and thanks to a product called Curl Free, was almost straight.

Makeup was big in Albuquerque, and my friends and I had been experimenting with it for a few years. Thick black eyeliner and a lot of mascara. I would sometimes draw Twiggy eyelashes, and I usually topped off the look with pale lipstick. I did the same today. David hadn't said anything about makeup, and since he was a guy maybe he wouldn't notice.

He didn't.

The dance party was located on the other side of town, in an area of flat-roofed houses with curved driveways and even a few trees. I got the sense that this was where the wealthy people lived.

I spotted a mailbox with balloons attached. David pulled to the curb and put the car in park. It was my mom's car. David didn't even have his own car. "Mr. Wallace is a chemist at the hospital," he said. "Mrs. Wallace is a substitute teacher at the grade school." I heard the approval in his voice.

I wanted to ask him how long I had to stay, but I remembered my vow of silence. I wouldn't speak to him unless I had to. Not because he'd commanded it, but because it was my choice, my decision.

I opened the door and gathered up the few albums I'd managed to find. It was a long way from the car to the house. Maybe I could make a run for it. Cut down an alley or something and hide. But I ached from the whipping. I didn't think I could move fast enough.

"I'll come to the door with you," he said as if suspecting an attempted getaway.

We walked up the sidewalk, and I tried to move at a normal gait, unwilling to give him the satisfaction of knowing he'd physically hurt me. He rang the doorbell. A smiling woman with short dark hair answered, and I could see that she liked David. I'll bet a lot of people liked him. They probably talked about how nice it was that he'd met a Catholic woman, and how nice it was that he was willing to marry her, even though she had kids.

"Come on in!" She swung the door wide. "Everybody's in the recreation room."

Recreation room. Yep. Wealthy.

"They are so excited!" she added.

I'd hoped nobody would be there. I wouldn't come to a party where some new girl was going to teach kids to dance. How uncool was that?

A boy about my age appeared, all smiles, wearing pressed beige slacks and a white shirt with a navy-blue tie. Short hair parted on the side. "We're all waiting!" he said. "Did you bring records?"

I handed him the few I'd gathered before leaving the house. Eric Burdon. Buffalo Springfield. The Zombies. "I'm still unpacking," I told him.

Introductions were made. A little conversation took place, then David said, "I'll be back in a few hours."

I followed the boy named Paul down the hallway and through a kitchen. The counter was covered with bowls of chips and plates of cookies. Glasses awaited juice and Kool-Aid. I hadn't eaten breakfast and I wanted to grab a cookie, but I restrained myself. This was obviously meant for later.

The boy led me to a big rectangular room. It was almost empty except for a few chairs, a stereo, and a banner that said "Welcome Theresa." At least it didn't say Welcome Theresa Balls.

There were about ten kids there, five girls, five boys, and they stood around and shyly waited for me to do something. Dance, I guess.

I wanted to disappear through the floor. The awkward silence grew.

"What kind of records do you have?" I finally asked.

Several of us swooped down on the stereo and began shuffling through albums. "I really don't know how to dance," I confessed. "I mean, I doubt I know anything more than you guys know."

A girl with long blond hair and white knee socks smiled sweetly. "We don't know any dances. A lot of people around here aren't even allowed to dance. And we can't have dances at school."

She had the strongest Southern accent I'd ever heard. Like somebody exaggerating and mocking a Southern accent.

"No school dances?" I was appalled.

"I love your hair," one of the girls said.

"I love your makeup," another added. "My parents won't let me wear makeup."

Paul put on an album, and we began to move around. The girls knew some basic steps, and the boys tried to follow along. But mostly we just talked. The girls wanted to know about makeup and music and radio stations.

"There are no good radio stations here," one of them said. "Sometimes at night you can pick up KOMA from Oklahoma City."

An hour later, I excused myself and made my way to the kitchen and food. I was relieved to find that the room was empty except for a boy I hadn't seen before. He was probably two or three years older than me, tall, with short curly hair.

"Are you here to teach me how to eat?" He picked up a chocolate-chip cookie and gave it a good eyeballing, as if trying to figure out how to put it in his mouth. "How about drinking a glass of Kool-Aid? I'm not sure how to do that either."

"Ha-ha," I said. "I didn't want to come."

"Sure. I'm Paul's brother, by the way. He was so excited about this whole deal." He shook his head at the thought of someone getting excited about me. "I wanted to see what kind of person had the nerve to blow into town like she was hot stuff."

I didn't owe him any explanation. I didn't care what he thought.

The mother appeared. She wore a yellow apron with red flowers. "Hello, dear," she said to the boy. "I thought you were helping your dad in the lab today." She grabbed a hot pad, opened the oven door, and removed a sheet of cookies. A gust of heat and the smell of chocolate wafted my way. My stomach growled, but the noise of the closing oven door covered it up.

The boy looked at me and smiled. "I had to meet the new girl in town."

"This is my eldest son, Noel." Mrs. Wallace rested the sheet on the stove, her back to us.

"Hi, Noel." I grabbed a cookie from a nearby plate and acted as if I couldn't find my mouth.

He let out a snort.

Mrs. Wallace swung around to the counter. "You seemed totally disinterested last night at dinner."

"I changed my mind."

She picked up a spatula. "Have a seat," she told me, motioning toward the table.

I looked at the wooden chairs and remembered how uncomfortable the car had been. "That's okay." I wolfed down the cookie.

"You're lucky to have such a wonderful father," she told me.

She knew my dad? Weird.

With the spatula, she began transferring cookies from the cookie sheet to a plate. "Try one of these. They're better right out of the oven."

Noel and I both grabbed one, the chocolate chips melting against our fingers.

"He's just the sweetest man," Mrs. Wallace said.

I finally realized she was talking about David.

"We were so excited when we heard he was getting married. You have no idea. We were afraid he'd always be a bachelor, and such a nice man deserves a nice wife and family. Funny how these things work out. I won't know what to do with myself now." She laughed, going on to explain, "I was always baking something for him. Almost every Sunday I took him a plate of food and dessert. Sometimes Noel would run it over for me."

I thought about the man who'd beaten me that morning. I thought about the man she knew. Had she made him out to be some sweet darling who couldn't take care of himself and who deserved to be babied, and he'd played along, lapped it up? Or had we changed him? In one day?

"But now he has a lovely new wife and two lovely children to take care of him."

Right. "Thanks for the snacks," I said to Mrs. Wallace. "And thanks for having me over."

She smiled like a real mom. *Was* she a real mom? Or was this a face she put on for strangers? Did she do weird things in private? Did she beat Noel and Paul? Did she shriek and sob, and lock herself in her bedroom? I didn't think so. I had the feeling this was who she was, the person standing right in front of me. I liked her. I almost wanted her to be my mother. I almost wanted to stay there and not go back home, ever. I imagined having my own room somewhere in their big house, and eating dinner at the table behind me.

The party ended, and David returned to pick me up. I wouldn't tell him I'd had a good time because that didn't matter. He didn't need to know, and he wouldn't care. None of this was about me.

"We're going to church at nine o'clock tomorrow morning," he said as we headed back to the little house on Juniper Street. "Even though you're grounded, I expect you to go with us, and I expect you to partake in communion."

We'd quit going to church years ago, and this was something new he'd brought into our lives. It was like he'd come equipped with a set of rules that he didn't question, rules we also had to follow even though they hadn't been written for us.

"And don't wear all of that makeup," he said.

So he *had* noticed.

"You look like a prostitute."

Tomorrow would be our first public appearance. He didn't want to drag a whore with him to church.

Chapter 12

A murmur followed us as we entered the church. I would have chosen to sit in back, but David, proud as a peacock, walked up the center aisle, my mother on his arm, my brother and I trailing behind. We took a seat a few rows from the altar.

The church was tiny, more like a plain country church. There was nothing ornate, no gold trim, no statues. Just white stucco walls and dark pews.

Shortly after we sat down, altar boys appeared in vestments. With golden staffs, they began lighting the staggered candles on either side of the altar. One of the boys was tall, with dark curly hair. Noel Wallace.

He never looked our direction. When communion rolled around, we lined up to lower ourselves to the red-velvet kneeler. Noel assisted the priest, holding the communion plate beneath the patrons' chins in case some crumble of God were to fall from a mouth and hit the floor. When it was my turn, I stuck out my tongue, opened my eyes, and stared at Noel.

He blinked and fumbled with the plate. The priest shot him a stern look as the communion wafer made contact with my tongue and vanished into my mouth. The wafer had an image of Jesus on it. Most people didn't know that, because we were supposed to keep our eyes closed. My actions were probably blasphemous, but I wasn't religious by choice. And now that David was forcing me to go to church, I planned on becoming even less religious. Maybe I wouldn't believe in God at all.

Once mass was over, people gathered outside. Old women sought us out in order to meet David's new family, and introductions were made again and again. It was hard for me to juggle my chill toward David with the warmth I would normally have used when meeting a bunch of gray-haired women in floral dresses. I probably came across as a surly teenager.

A pencil-thin, elegant woman with a cap of short black hair gave us a friendly hello. Her name was Julie and she coaxed me to the side with a smile and a hand on my arm.

"I'm looking for a sitter," she told me. She had a lovely Southern accent, not New Mexico, but more like Louisiana, and she had the sweetest, most beautiful face.

"My mother has dementia, poor dear, and it would be so delightful to be able to go out one night a week. I heard that you watch your brother, and I wondered if you'd be interested in sitting with my mother this Thursday. She's usually no trouble at all. She gets a little confused, but you'd just need to feed her, give her medicine, and put her to bed."

I had my doubts about taking care of an adult, but getting away from David and my mother for a few hours would be nice. "I'm sorry. I wouldn't be able to come for a while," I said. "I'm grounded."

"Oh, that's too bad. And you just got here!"

She probably wondered what kind of crime I'd committed, and maybe she wondered if she wanted a delinquent taking care of her mother.

David overheard the conversation and broke in. "We're making some exceptions," he said while my mother shot me a death-ray. "She'd be happy to come. I can even drop her off."

"Oh, that would be wonderful!" Julie clapped her white gloves together.

For someone who was grounded, my social calendar was filling fast.

Chapter 13

The high school was a mile from our house, my brother's school in the opposite direction. On that first Monday, we all headed out. David rode his bicycle to the college, my mother drove Jude to grade school, and I walked. My classes had already been set up, and all I had to do was check in at the office. Artesia High School contained four grades, nine through twelve, and some of those classes were mixed, combining all ages.

I missed my first class, math, but made it to my second, art.

According to the map I'd been given, art class was held in a detached building that housed both art and shop. I found it easily, and entered as soon as the previous class exited.

Cement floor. Long, narrow tables with tall metal stools. Windows that let in a lot of light, and the teacher's glassed office in one corner. The room smelled like clay and paint and wood. The lady in the office told me most classes didn't have assigned seating, so I placed my books on a table and sat down, my back to the wall so I could watch kids file in. Many hung out in the hallway, laughing and talking, waiting for class to begin.

I hated this. Hated being the new kid.

"Hey. You."

It took a moment to realize the guy was talking to me. The words came from a big Mexican with long, dark hair and an orange peace sign on his dingy T-shirt. "I heard about you," he said. "Heard about how you think you're so much better than everybody. Teaching kids to dance." He rolled his eyes. "And I've seen your dad around, riding his bicycle to the college."

The guy was like a huge, angry bear. He probably weighed at least two hundred pounds. He didn't know me, but he hated me. The words *to the college* seemed to have a hidden message I wasn't picking up on.

An audience of students began to gather, a mob of faces, arms clutching books.

I wanted them to vanish. I wanted to go home, lock the door to my bedroom, and crawl under the covers and never come out. But that wouldn't be enough. That wouldn't last. Being dead. That would last. That would get me out of here.

Like a lot of teenagers, I fantasized about killing myself. But I could never tie a rope to a beam and kick the chair out from under me. I could never shoot myself in the head. Maybe I could slit my wrists. Maybe, but even that didn't seem appealing. Pills. That would be the way to go. Like Marilyn Monroe. If someone handed me a bottle of pills today, tonight, would I take them?

I didn't like the idea of David and my mother finding me. I didn't want them standing over me when I could no longer defend myself even if I were dead. Totally at their mercy. If I killed myself I'd have to go away. I'd walk into the desert and do it. Or hide in a culvert somewhere, and when the spring rains came my rotten carcass would be swept into the street. That wasn't appealing either.

I wanted to hit a switch and make it all stop.

A willowy Mexican girl in a short white skirt stepped forward. "Leave her alone, Ruben."

He glanced to the side, then back at me as if afraid to break away for too long. "This is none of your business," he told the girl.

"I said, leave her alone."

She was fearless and matter-of-fact, her tone one a mother might use on a kid. But he didn't seem like a kid; he seemed like a mean, grumpy man. He had dark hair on his face. Not a beard, but a lot of straggly stuff, as if he shaved, but not all the time. Some bully who'd flunked a few grades and was somehow still in school.

I didn't understand his hostility.

"I can't decide which one of you to hate the most," Ruben said. "You—" he pointed at me, "—for thinking you are better than us. Or you—" he pointed to the girl in the white skirt, "—for sticking up for her." He wagged his fingers between us, as if trying to decide. "You … or you?"

I was aware of open mouths and big eyes, the stunned silence of the room. Without thought, I jumped to my feet and threw one hand high in the air. I bounced like a crazy woman in a game show. "Ooh, ooh! Pick me! Pick me!"

The room exploded. Or was it my head? No, the sound was laughter. Students clutched their stomachs, knees bent as they almost collapsed.

The big guy who'd started the attack stared at me with shock that slowly changed to anger, followed by annoyance, followed by a reluctant smile. Then he turned and walked away and the crowd dispersed.

The girl who'd come to my defense stepped closer. "Ruben's brother died a few months ago in Vietnam. He's been hard to deal with ever since."

"That's awful." I glanced away long enough to see Ruben plop down in the corner, a sullen expression on his face. "So he takes out his pain on other people?"

"It's the college that set him off." The girl had a beautiful Spanish accent, almond-shaped eyes with long, black lashes, and perfect skin. "Your dad teaches there?" she asked.

"Not my dad, but ... well ..." What did I call David when talking about him to other people? "Stepdad." It was easier that way. Easier than saying the weirdo my mother married.

"A lot of people around here hate the college," she explained. "Rich white kids coming to town in their fancy cars, getting out of the draft because Daddy paid to send them to a pretend school."

Pretend school. There it was again.

"Ruben figures if his brother could have paid to go to college he'd be alive right now."

I understood Ruben's anger, but why pick on me? I had nothing to do with it. But this was another piece of information about David I didn't like. If what people said about the school was true, did it mean David was okay with it?

"I've heard teachers give the students whatever grades they need to keep up their deferment status," the girl said.

"I don't think David would do that." But he might look the other way if something like that were happening. He'd be oblivious to it, the way he was oblivious to some of my mother's behavior.

"If it's true, the rich boys' fathers pay to keep their precious sons from going to Vietnam, and pay for a degree at the same time. Must be nice. Oh, my name's Winona. I like your hair. We can be twins." She laughed, and I could tell she was laughing at the idea of our being twins. She gave me a smile, and glided across the room, taking a seat at Ruben's table.

I returned to the metal stool and opened a spiral notebook, staring at a blank page, pretending to read as I waited for my heart to quit pounding. This was a whole new world. Two hundred and fifty miles from Albuquerque, but it felt like a foreign country.

Someone took a seat across from me; I looked up to see Noel Wallace. Was he everywhere? "You have art class second hour?" I asked in disbelief. I couldn't deal with him right now. I glanced away, looking for another table. Winona and Ruben? But that would be rude of me to leave.

"Does that seem strange?" he asked. "For me to take art?"

I tried to settle into the idea of a conversation with this annoying guy. "You seem more like the science type. Or literature type. Or civics type."

"I do like to read." He went through his stack of books and pulled out a paperback. *Stranger in a Strange Land.*

"I'm reading that right now," I said. "I'm about half done."

"Really." He was looking at me with interest, as if seeing me in a different light. We talked about the plot for a few minutes, made a few *grok* jokes, then Noel said, "Close your eyes."

"No."

"You have lines on your eyelids."

I closed them. A second later, I felt his finger moving across the crease of one lid, then the other, smoothing the eye shadow. "There. I don't know why you wear all that makeup."

I shrugged. "I'm used to it. It's part of me."

"You weren't wearing any yesterday at church. You looked pretty without it. Is it a mask? Armor? Some tribes paint their faces when they go into battle."

He was trying to be funny, but makeup did make me feel safer. It made me feel hard and strong. "I've heard soldiers in Vietnam paint their faces," I said.

"I've heard that too."

"Would you ever go to Vietnam?"

"I'll be eligible in less than two years."

I was instantly afraid for him. "Maybe the war will be over by then."

"Maybe. I saw what happened with Ruben. A lot of people in this town have lost family in Vietnam. One day I wore a black armband to school to protest, and my science teacher left the room in tears. He just broke down. I'll never forget the look on his face. Turned out his son had just died over there. You don't think about that kind of thing, like how it touches almost everybody you run into."

I'd never known anyone who'd been impacted by Vietnam. It was just something I heard about on the news and in music. The riots, the protests. But now I seemed surrounded by it.

Someone cleared his throat. I looked up to see a short man with bushy hair and a bushy mustache. "I hate to interrupt," he said, "but if you hadn't noticed, class has started."

Noel straightened his posture and clasped his hands in his lap. "Sorry, Mr. G."

Noel. He was growing on me. I got the feeling I could trust him. He reminded me of my older brother without the meanness.

Chapter 14

There was no easing into this new life. One day we lived in Albuquerque with no adult male in our lives, the next we were living with a stranger in a tiny house in southern New Mexico.

Overnight, our mother was preparing meals and wearing an apron. And it would have been fine, it would have been great, if not for this peculiar man in our midst and the feeling that none of this was real, that it was all an act, that some alien had crept into my mother's skin while she slept, and this new person, someone I didn't know or recognize, had taken her place. The whole thing seemed like a parody of our old life, the Florida life. And it almost seemed that this was something my mother was doing to get back at my father, to teach him a lesson, to show him that she could have a husband and a life without him.

But what she didn't get was that my father didn't care. He wasn't paying attention to any of us. He didn't even know that she was trying to erase him.

What was my dad doing now? I wondered. Right this minute. I knew that he and Eve were still living in California. And they still had servants and a mansion and Rolls-Royces.

In my mind, my dad never got any older. I always pictured him at a party, a drink in his hand, laughing and talking to beautiful women in sleek dresses and pearl necklaces. Off in the distance, music played and a chef in a white jacket cooked a fancy dinner, while tapered candles lit a long table. Outside a sliding glass door, the swimming pool shimmered. Beyond that, where the yard dipped to a retaining wall, the lights of Los Angeles twinkled. The old lady with her swept-back hair would appear, and in an exotic accent she would call him dear and sweetheart and darling. That's how I always pictured him. Happy, surrounded by wealth. I suppose it might be easier to accept the wrongness of a situation when the setting was so lovely.

Now, as I watched my mother's attempts at what seemed an imitation of life, I wondered if there was only one real path, and once you veered from it you were basically just acting, just pretending. All the other paths were cheap imitations, some more disturbing than others. In the end, it wouldn't have mattered who my mother had married, because none of them would be my father. And David seemed harmless. And never had a woman been so cherished.

"I'm hot," she would say. And David would dash away, knees bent, arms extended, scurrying around to find a fan. "I'm cold." he would dash off to find a blanket. "I have a headache." He would let out a broken whimper, and run to the kitchen for a glass of water and two aspirin. He would have chewed her food if she'd asked him. He would have killed the neighbor if she'd asked him. He would have loved my brother and me if she'd told him to, and he would have bludgeoned us to death if she'd commanded it, all the while smiling and asking if he was killing us right. But a person without a thought of his own could be dangerous in unexpected ways. My mother became the cult leader, and David became her devoted follower, and together they were their own little cult of two.

David adored my mother. Unlike my father, David would never leave her. Was that another reason to marry him? An ex-Christian Brother who would be as dedicated to his new wife as he was to God? David would never walk out on her. He would never leave her to fend for herself, or leave her for another woman. He would never get tired of her, bored with her. He would adore her more with every passing day.

And in return, my mother would mold him, and he would like what she liked, eat what she ate, drink what she drank, believe what she believed, read what she read, love and hate what and whom she loved and hated. I'd never been around a person so ... empty. Blank. David was like a robot she'd found and brought home, a robot who would gradually learn her ways, who would mimic and absorb and reflect an image of her humanity, but it was easy to see he would never be truly human. There was some basic ingredient that didn't exist in him. Maybe it had never been there, or maybe it had been wiped away by the sheltered life he'd led, having been put in the monastery at age twelve.

I didn't understand why my mother married David, but I also didn't understand why he'd married her. This wasn't love. Was it? It was some weird, twisted worship. She was his god and his wife and his mother, all wrapped into one.

She dove into the role, and the only time she broke character was when she happened to look at me, when our eyes met and our gazes didn't flit away to take in our new surroundings. When there was a brief lock, a connection, and I could see the truth in her heart.

A fraction of a second later, she would look away and go back to whatever domestic chore she was performing, once again the devoted wife of a college professor. But in that brief second, I saw the terror embedded deep in her eyes, and the question: *What have I done?*

Chapter 15

Julie filled me in on her mother's care as we drove across town. The elegant woman I'd met at church was wearing a black dress and black tights and black shoes. Her black hair was straight and short, and the only makeup on her face was red lipstick. She looked and sounded like somebody who might be in theater, or who might read poetry in a dark bar, and smoke with a long cigarette holder. "I took my mother to specialist after specialist," she said, guiding the car over bumpy streets. "And finally, in New Orleans, where I was living when she got sick, they told me she had something called Alzheimer's disease."

Here I thought I'd just be hanging around with an elderly woman. In my mind I'd pictured my grandmother, and I'd already hoped Julie's mother and I might play cards. Preferably Gin Rummy. Now

I suddenly imagined myself wearing a doctor's mask in a room that was pale green and smelling of urine and bleach.

"Is it contagious?" I asked. I didn't want to catch a disease.

"It's nothing like that." Her voice went flat, and I got the idea she didn't really want to explain it to me. Maybe it was too painful.

"It's a mental disorder, and sometimes she gets a little confused," Julie said. "That's all. I've had a few older women come and sit with her, but she didn't like them, so I thought it might be a good idea to try someone young. But don't take it personally if she doesn't like you. That's just the disease. Strangers sometimes upset her."

I didn't understand how confusion was a disease. Maybe Julie just didn't want to say her mother was crazy.

"All you have to do is keep her company and make sure she takes her sleeping pill before going to bed."

The woman's name was Estelle, and her hand, when she greeted me, was like a bird claw covered with tissue paper. I could feel her brittle bones, and I could see the blue, protruding veins wrapped around the smooth white of her knuckles. She smelled like mouthwash and old books, and she clung to me like I was the youth she'd lost, and maybe the youth she could recapture if she held me long enough, and stared at me hard enough, the frantic pressure of her fingertips transmitting a fear of where she was going, and an unwillingness to go there alone. Even though she scared me, I felt an unexpected connection. This wasn't a card-playing grandmother, or a crazy person. Behind her eyes, I could see her mind working, see the life there, and I could feel the energy of a life that was different from the energy of the foyer where we stood.

She wanted me to come with her. To her world.

She gave me a shy smile, and I realized she still clung to my hand, and the silent communication suddenly seemed a secret between the two of us. Estelle was looking at me like someone who'd been waiting a long time for a playmate, and here I was.

People said the woman at the Dairy Queen was a witch. She didn't look like a witch except for the missing teeth. She had blond hair, and she smelled like cigarette smoke and old bowling-alley shoes. One day she handed me an ice-cream cone, gasped, and through the little sliding window she grabbed my hand in much the same way the old woman was doing now.

"You're a sensitive." She watched me with fevered eyes and a tilt to her head, as if listening to some invisible person whispering to her from far away.

"I just want some ice cream," I'd said.

"You have power," the blond witch told me. Refrigerated air blasted through the window, and I could smell stainless steel and sour milk. She handed me a cone and slid the window shut. As I lipped off the curl, I glanced up to see her watching me through the blurry glass. She nodded. I didn't.

Once I got home, I looked up the word *sensitive* and found that it meant I could sense what others were feeling and thinking. I rather liked the idea of being someone who was in-tune to other people, but I also knew my skill was something I'd learned growing up with a mother who wore many faces and came wrapped in many moods, most of them dark. You learned to read people after a while. Anybody could do it. And yet I couldn't help but feel special knowing the witch at the Dairy Queen had picked up on my talent. When she'd looked at me, I got the feeling she knew everything there was to know about me. Like who I would marry, and how many kids I would have, and when I would die. Nobody had ever looked at me like that.

Estelle released my hand. I felt sure we would get along. Not only get along, but I would be her co-conspirator.

"Theresa is here to keep you company tonight," Julie said in a voice meant to cheer, coerce, and sidestep any unforeseen conflict. As a group, we moved out of the foyer.

The short entryway led to a living room and couch. The wall above the couch was covered with framed drawings that were all by the same artist, signed with a flourish I couldn't decipher. Most of the drawings were of people. One woman who could have been Estelle sat at an outdoor café, in the kind of place I'd never been but had seen in movies.

To the right of the living room was a kitchen counter with stools, and, behind that, a sink, stove, and refrigerator, all a sick yellow. It was more like an apartment than a house. Through sliding glass doors, I saw a cement patio and fenced yard.

Julie gave me instructions about dinner and the nightly routine, and then she was gone, leaving me alone with the little woman.

Estelle knew the routine of the evening. She shuffled around the kitchen, helping to get our meal, humming happily as we stood side by side, preparing a sandwich that I sliced in two, corner to corner. She seemed pretty normal to me.

"Would you like to sit in the backyard?" she asked, falling into the role of hostess. "It's lovely this time of the day."

I carried a tray outside, and we sat at a glass-topped table on the patio. The chairs were metal with an overlay of white paint, and the seats were cold and springy. The meal was a half sandwich each, chips, red grapes, and lemonade, all easy on the stomach.

"Remember that trip to Paris?" Estelle asked, as she dabbed a napkin against her lips. Her wrinkled cheeks were two bright spots of rouge, and her nose was dull with white powder, hastily and blindly applied. "Right after you graduated from college?"

"Paris?" I asked, thinking I'd missed part of the conversation in my perusal of her wrinkled cheeks.

"We sat on the patio and fed the pigeons. Remember? Oh, that was the loveliest day! And you were wearing the blue sweater I bought for you at that cute little shop. It looked so good with your brown hair."

It was the weirdest thing going from thinking she was perfectly normal to knowing she wasn't normal at all.

Sometimes she gets a little confused.

"What's my name?" I asked with caution.

"Josephine."

I shook my head. "I'm not Josephine."

"You are!" Like a child having a tantrum, she tossed sandwich crust. It missed her plate, and dropped to the cement patio. When I bent to pick it up, she told me to leave it. The dog would get it. There was no dog.

"Why would you say you aren't Josephine?" She frowned and leaned closer, staring at me, reading my face. "You *are* Josephine!" Her eyes became hostile and suspicious. "And if you aren't, then who are you? And what are you doing in my house?" She braced her hands on the arms of the metal chair, threatening to take action. "I should call the police. That's what I should do. I should call the police and tell them some strange person is in my house, eating my food."

"Okay, I'm Josephine." I tried to keep my voice light even though my heart was pounding. "I just got mixed up for a minute."

She settled back in her seat. "I don't know why you would pull such a trick on your own mother, but then you always did have an ornery streak." She relaxed, but I could see she hadn't quite forgiven me.

Her daughter. So Josephine was one of her daughters. "I'm sorry. That was a bad joke."

"Yes, it was."

"Let's just forget about it and enjoy our dinner."

The word dinner seemed to stir a clock inside her head. "You'll still be here tomorrow, won't you?"

"If I'm not, Julie will be home."

"Who's Julie?"

"You're other daughter."

"You're my only daughter. I just have one child."

I couldn't help but think about my dad, someone who'd deliberately forgotten his kids. And here was this poor woman who couldn't remember hers. But I didn't think it was my place to set her straight about how many daughters she had.

Sometimes I look at a stranger, maybe someone in a passing car or someone in the grocery store, and I wonder what that person's life is like. And I imagine being that person, imagine returning home to unpack my groceries while my children cluster around me, everyone smiling.

I could pretend to be Estelle's daughter.

We talked about Paris and the trips we'd taken together. We talked about my art degree and what I would do now that I'd graduated. With Estelle, I was able to step into a role and pretend to have a relationship I'd never had with my own mother. I could be the adored daughter. I didn't feel bad about playing along, not for Estelle anyway. But for me, I wondered if it was as much about creating something I didn't have, as it was trying to reassure an old, sick woman.

The sky grew dark and we gathered up the plates and went inside. Estelle watched television while I did the dishes. After that, she brushed her teeth and put on a nightgown, then got into bed.

"Here's your medicine."

She plucked the pill from my palm and washed it down with a glass of water, then passed the glass back. On a dresser was a framed photo of Julie and a woman with brown hair that I assumed was Josephine. They were both smiling at the camera. Had Estelle taken the picture? I picked up the photo and turned it toward the woman in bed. I pointed to Julie. "Who's this?" I asked in a casual voice.

She leaned forward and frowned, then fell back against the pillow. "I don't know."

"And this?" I pointed to the woman with brown hair.

"Why, that's Josephine. That's you. What a silly question."

I replaced the photo, turned on the bedside lamp, and turned off the harsh ceiling light. "How about if I read to you?" I asked.

I left her for a moment to find a book, then returned to settle into a chair next to the bed. By the time I opened to the first page of *Wuthering Heights*, her eyelids were getting heavy. Two pages in, she was sound asleep.

"She thought I was her daughter," I told Julie once she returned a couple of hours later. She paused as she hung her sweater in the closet near the front door, a question on her face.

"Josephine," I explained, but I could already see this was going down a bad road.

"Josephine?" she asked weakly, her arms dropping as if all the strength had been sucked out of her. "She thought you were Josephine?"

I wished I hadn't said anything. This was the secret Estelle hadn't wanted me to reveal.

"Josephine is dead," Julie said, moving slowly toward the kitchen, grabbing blindly for a stool and sitting down. I'd spoiled her evening. I'd spoiled her few hours out.

"She died five years ago."

I didn't want her to know I'd pretended to be Josephine. Here was Estelle, someone who adored and missed her dead daughter so much that she'd brought her back from the dead, while at the same time no longer recognizing the living daughter right in front of her. What an odd, horrible disease.

"Josephine had just gotten her degree in art," Julie said. "You probably noticed the drawings everywhere. Those are hers."

From her shoulder bag, Julie produced a pack of cigarettes, shook one out, lit it, and tossed the smoking match into an orange ashtray shaped like a giant leaf. "She and my mother took a trip to Paris." She fiddled with the book of matches, not looking at me. "I was supposed to go with them, but decided I couldn't afford it. Anyway, they took a cab from the airport and were in a car wreck. Josephine was killed instantly."

I didn't know what to say. I was a kid. A kid who'd just spent the past few hours pretending to be Julie's dead sister.

"It's so strange, you know. How my mother has rewritten her past. I don't even exist, and yet she thinks Josephine is still alive. It's like the Alzheimer's has given Josephine back to her, but taken me away. I'm glad she has Josephine back. I wish I could have Josephine back, but why doesn't she know me? And I can't get mad. That's what's so frustrating. How can I get mad at her? She's hurting me. She's killing me, and she doesn't even know it. This is such a heartless disease. Sometimes I don't know how much longer I can stand it. Everybody says this is what I should be doing. I'm her daughter. And even I say this is what I should be doing. But before I came, I imagined sharing meaningful moments." She let out a harsh laugh. "There are no meaningful moments."

At the sink, I filled a glass with water and slid it to her, then pulled up a stool for myself. Maybe because I was a kid she felt like she could unload. Or maybe she simply had no one else to talk to.

She took a drink, then continued, "I knew there would be more memory loss as time passed, but I didn't think she'd completely forget me while remembering my sister. Don't get me wrong. I loved my sister. I adored her. I miss her every single day. But this. This is more than my mind can bear. Alzheimer's is cruel in ways you can't imagine. And nobody understands. I don't even know anybody else who is going through this or who has gone through it."

I'd had an enjoyable evening. I'd even thought it was fun. To pretend. To get away from the darkness of my own house and life. To pretend I was the adored daughter of a sweet old woman. I had no emotional ties to Estelle. There was nothing to hurt me here. No way to inflict pain. I could pretend. I could sip imaginary tea and talk about a trip to Paris I'd never really taken. And I could enjoy it. I had nothing at stake here. I'd never known the person Estelle was before. And I could tell her I loved her because they were just the words I spoke to make her feel better. Of course I didn't love her. Odd, that it was sometimes easier to say things when you didn't mean them.

But poor Julie.

Every word her mother spoke cut her to the bone. Even the evening out hadn't helped.

"Will she get better?" I asked. Of course she would. What a silly question.

Julie shook her head. "Doctors can't say how long she'll be like this, but she'll continue to fade until she can't even talk or feed herself."

I didn't understand how a disease could do such a thing.

"I think I made a mistake moving here." Julie took a long drag from her cigarette, then blew smoke at the ceiling. "But have you ever been to one of those places?"

"You mean a nursing home? No."

"They're horrible. I can't imagine putting her in one. So what else could I do? I really had no choice. I haven't told anybody this, but I don't even like her anymore. That woman in there, that person who yells at me all day long, she's not my mother. My mother is gone. I've given up my life to take care of her, but I'm too exhausted to figure out where to go from here. What do we owe our parents? If my mother were still with me rather than that imposter, what would she want me to do? I know she wouldn't approve of this situation. I know she would probably tell me to put her in a home, or leave a glass of poison next to the bed." Julie gasped and put a hand to her mouth, shocked by her own words.

But I kind of got it. I kind of understood.

From outside, a horn honked. Two quick toots. David. "That's my ride," I said, sliding off the kitchen stool. I hesitated a moment, hoping Julie would remember to pay me. She didn't, and I hated to ask. Not now.

"Call if you want me to come again," I said.

"Oh, I will. Next Thursday."

Would I be Josephine? If so, I wouldn't tell Julie. I wouldn't mention her dead sister at all.

At home, I asked my mother if she'd ever heard of Alzheimer's.

"No."

At school, I asked classmates and teachers.

"No."

"Just sounds like a fancy name for crazy to me," said the neighbor guy down the street.

Maybe he was right. Maybe the death of Josephine had sent Estelle over the edge. Whatever the cause, not a single person had heard of the disease, and with relief I decided that Alzheimer's must be rare. I would never get it, and nobody in my family would ever get it. And in a few years doctors would have a cure.

Chapter 16

The phone on the kitchen wall rang and my mother answered it. After a brief listen, she handed the receiver to me. This was one of her good days. She'd gone out to lunch with a group of faculty wives, and she'd been in a state of euphoria since returning home. Tomorrow the crash would come, but for now we could relax. These were the hours that made life tolerable. Our days were filled with dread, but also hope. And when the good days came, they were wonderful gifts. Tonight, we would all four sit around the table and talk and laugh. For a little while we would be a normal family. Maybe better than a normal family because this was, in some odd way, a reward for everything that had gone before.

The phone in my hand was a modern design called a Slimline, and the color matched the avocado green of the cupboards, stove, and refrigerator. It had a long rubber cord, curled, also avocado. When stretched, it could reach out the front or back door. Sometimes, like now, it was too tangled to uncoil, and instead kept the user tethered close to the wall.

The voice at the other end belonged to a young man. Randy, from my art class. He always arrived in his orange and white letter jacket, big shoulders, and blond hair perfectly parted. He was a senior, and captain of the football team. I tried not to hold that against him.

Artesia was home of the Bulldogs, and the high-school football team had been state champions several years in a row, so many years that failure was now out of the question. Winning was no longer about celebration, but a need to keep shame at bay. The town had little to brag about, and the football team *was* Artesia, and orange and white were the town colors. The orange wasn't a nice pumpkin orange, but a shade of that made a person uneasy. A shade that said road construction, a shade that didn't belong on the broad side of a building, and didn't belong on house trim or storefronts or flagpoles.

I had no idea why Randy would call my house. Did this have something to do with art class? Had I dropped something? Had he found it? Had he dialed my number by mistake?

He asked how I was, what I was doing. Over the phone, his Southern accent was even more pronounced. Instead of a football jersey, I suddenly imagined him holding a guitar, wearing a western shirt with pearl buttons and fringe.

I was uncomfortably aware of my mother standing at the stove, stirring chocolate sauce with a wooden spoon. My stepfather sat at the table that was also avocado green, reading the paper and waiting for the meal to be served. Every once in a while he would sniff the air in appreciation and toss an encouragement to my mother. "That sure smells good." And, "I can't wait."

I tried to untangle the phone cord so I could step outside, but it would require that I put down the receiver and work at the mess with both hands, so I gave up.

"I wondered if you'd like to go out," Randy said.

"Out?" Was this some kind of local jargon I didn't yet understand?

"To eat and to a movie." He sounded sweetly
nervous, and I finally realized he was asking me on a
date. I'd never been on a date, and I'd never been
asked out on a date. Dates were things my mother
did. Thing adults did. And why would the captain of
the football team be interested in me? I would have
thought this was a prank, but he didn't seem the type
for pranks.

I hunched my shoulders over the phone, face to
the wall, cupping the receiver in both hands, trying to
create a sense of privacy. "Are you sure you have the
right number?"

He laughed. And then I remembered he was
always laughing at the things I said. I appreciated that.

He was waiting for an answer.

"I'm grounded." Being grounded could work in
my favor, could make this awkward situation easier to
deal with.

My mother tapped me on the shoulder and I
turned. *Who is it?* she mouthed.

I covered the circle of holes in the plastic phone,
then, to add another layer of insulation, pressed the
phone to my stomach. I told her who was calling.
"He's asking me on a date." I stared at her in panic. A

date. At that moment, I realized I was looking at my mother, hoping for help. From my mother.

"You can go," she whispered.

No, I mouthed, and shook my head, hoping she would understand and back me up. "I'm grounded," I reminded her.

"We'll allow you to go."

"I don't want to," I whispered.

What should I do? He'd sounded so nervous. It had taken guts to give me a call. What a horrible situation for someone to put himself in. I wondered what his home life was like. I'll bet his parents were normal. I wondered what he'd think if he knew what mine were like. His call was a harsh intrusion into a world he could be no part of, an innocent reminder of the difference between me and my classmates.

I pulled my sweaty hand from the mouthpiece. When I talked into the plastic, I smelled my mother's breath, trapped in the tiny holes, and I could smell David too, down in that darkness, but mostly my mother. "Randy ... I ... um, can't go."

Beside me, my mother gestured frantically, nodding, telling me it was okay, that I should do it.

"Why?" Randy's nervousness dropped away to be replaced by disbelief.

"I just don't think it would be a good idea," I said.

"Oh." He was stunned, and I wondered if he'd ever been turned down. Maybe rejection was a good thing for him to experience.

"I'm really sorry," I said. "It was nice of you to ask." He would hate me now. He wouldn't smile at me, and he wouldn't laugh at my jokes. I tried to think of something funny to say, but couldn't. "See you tomorrow."

I hung up.

"What are you doing?" my mother said. "I said you could go."

"I didn't want to. He's captain of the football team." I waited for her to understand. When she didn't, I elaborated, "You always made fun of sports and football. And he's a senior. He's too old for me. And I don't even know him. I have no idea why he'd ask me out."

"He obviously finds you attractive," David said. As soon as he spoke, he realized he'd given me a compliment. He shot my mother a guilty look and vanished behind the paper again.

I didn't get it. The whole dating thing. I hadn't even thought my mother and David would allow me to date, but apparently they were impressed by letter jackets and football stars.

At school the next day, groups of girls glanced my direction; heads turned, hands covered whispering mouths. I did a finger-check of my hair. I checked to make sure my skirt wasn't trapped in my underwear, or that I didn't have toilet paper stuck to my shoe.

On the sidewalk that led from the main building to the art annex, Winona swooped up behind me and grabbed my arm, leaning in close. She smelled like tortillas and baby powder, and I figured she'd probably changed her little sister's diaper before school. "I can't believe you didn't say you'd go out with Randy Thompson!" She dragged me off the sidewalk and around the corner. "Tell me it's not true. Tell me he didn't ask you out, and tell me you didn't say no."

"Why would I go out with him?"

"The whole school's talking about it. He broke up with his girlfriend a week ago," Winona said. "People have been wondering who he'll ask out. Almost everybody thought it would be April Victor, the head cheerleader."

"So as soon as he breaks up with one girl, he needs another?"

I started walking toward the art building and Winona fell into step beside me.

"You don't get it," she said. "Every girl in the school is dying to go out with him."

"Not every girl."

She stopped. "There he is."

He stood on the sidewalk, smiling down at a dark-haired young woman in a red skirt and saddle shoes. April Victor. She was wearing his letter jacket.

"Wow. That didn't take long," I said.

"It could have been you," Winona reminded me.

"That's what I was afraid of."

"You're crazy."

Inside art class, we sat at a table with Noel. All three of us worked on clay sculptures while waiting for a free potting wheel.

Randy entered the room. Without looking my direction, he took a seat at a table at the far end of the rectangular room.

"Heard you broke that guy's heart," Noel said, picking up a sculpting tool with a mental loop at one end.

"I don't know how you can break someone's heart if you don't even know him." I rolled a small ball of clay between my fingers, then placed it on the head in front of me, above the eye socket of my masterpiece. "I mean, he seems like a nice guy, but ... he's a football player. I don't even know what we'd talk about."

"What about me?" Noel asked.

"What do you mean?"

"Would you go out with me? Would you like to try to break my heart?"

I thought about the first time we'd met at the dance party. That seemed months ago, but it had only been three weeks. Since then, we'd spent art class bickering in a good-natured way, but I'd certainly never thought of him as boyfriend material. I'd never thought of anybody as boyfriend material. In the back of my mind, I understood that my mother's failed relationships played a part in my lack of interest in the opposite sex. I liked to think I was the one who wasn't allowing myself to become caught up in social expectations. But maybe there was something wrong with me. Maybe I should have wanted to go out with Randy Thompson.

I concentrated on my sculpture, molding and shaping an eyebrow with my fingers. A bust of a man. I had no idea who I was creating. A face. Just a face.

But sometimes I thought it looked too much like my father.

"You should go out with Noel," Winona said as she rolled out a long piece of clay for her freehand pot.

"Just a minute ago you said I should go out with Randy," I reminded her. "And Noel's just kidding about going out."

"I'm serious," Noel said. "This weekend."

My heart beat faster. "My parents won't let me."

"They know me. I'll bet they will."

The idea of dating, no matter who was involved, seemed wrong. It implied that I would share things with a special person, details of my life, things I wanted no one to know. It implied that we might hold hands or kiss. Or more. It implied that he would buy things for me, a movie, food, and I would owe him something in return. A kiss. Or more. It came with a sense of ownership. The boys owned the girls. David owned my mother. Even though he did everything she said, he still owned her.

All along I'd thought Noel disliked me, or barely tolerated me. This was going to take a mental adjustment.

"I'll call your stepdad and ask him," Noel offered.

Noel went to our church. He was an altar boy. David would say yes.

I couldn't believe I was thinking about going out with Noel, my nemesis. At the same time, I hadn't been allowed to go anywhere since we'd moved to Artesia. School and church and right after supper, my tiny bedroom. I was a prisoner. I was fourteen, and couldn't do anything. Sometimes I imagined myself held captive in a tower. Oddly enough, this dream involved a handsome prince coming to the rescue. But rescue was different than ownership. In the daydream, the relationship always ended with the rescue. The escape followed by galloping away on a white horse. In reality, I would walk out the front door and get into a tan Chevy and we would go bowling. And then I would return to prison. I knew this was going to be my life, so I needed to have as much fun and live as much as I could in those few hours of freedom. And Noel would help me. Maybe I would even tell him a little of what went on behind the walls of our house.

Chapter 17

"Pull the smoke deep into your lungs, hold it as long as you can, then exhale slowly," Noel said.

So much for thinking he and I would go bowling or to the A&W for a strawberry shake. My mother and David were thrilled when I told them Noel had asked me out, so I couldn't help feeling that this moment had come with their giant stamp of approval. A nice Catholic boy, an altar boy, teaching me how to smoke pot. I'd been around marijuana once in Albuquerque, at a neighbor's house, but I'd just watched some people smoke it, then walked home in the dark feeling as if I'd witnessed something strange and daring and scary and wonderful. But mostly scary.

Noel and I were sitting in the backseat of James's car; James and his girlfriend were in the front seat. James was eighteen and had dropped out of high school to work at his dad's gas station. I'd only met him two hours ago, but I knew he was obsessed with cars. The car we were in was a GTO.

"My dad and I have been working on the engine," he'd told us. Then he'd launched into an explanation of what they'd done to give it more power, stuff about carburetors and cams and things that made no sense to me. His dad had supplied the beer we were drinking. I didn't know where the marijuana had come from.

"Still having a little problem with the ignition," James said. "We put a new one in today, and it's not catching every time."

I briefly worried about how I would smell when I got home, but then I tried to quit thinking about it. This was my first night of freedom. I wanted to have fun.

The pot burned my throat, so I took a swallow of beer. I knew what beer tasted like. My grandmother was German, and she'd sometimes give me a tiny glass of beer if she was having a drink. "You have to know what beer tastes like," she'd tell me.

I usually took a few sips and that was it. I liked the foam, but I didn't like the bitterness. But now the alcohol cooled my burning throat. The joint was coming back around. When it got to me, I shook my head. "I'll stick with beer."

We were in Roswell, a town forty miles north of Artesia. I liked that there was a lot of distance between my mother and me. No way could she find me here. It was dark, and we were parked somewhere outside of town at the end of a dirt road. James had turned the car around so we were facing the way we'd come in. There'd been some discussion about whether he should shut the engine off, but he'd finally decided to take the chance. "We can push-start it if we have to," he'd said.

We were going to a movie. *Rosemary's Baby*. I didn't know how we could go to a movie drunk and stoned. That seemed like a bad idea. Especially a scary movie.

James's girlfriend went to Artesia High School. Her name was Mandy. I didn't have any classes with her, but I'd seen her in the hallway. She was always tidy, kind of a geek with big glasses and dresses that were too long, paired with white knee socks. It was odd to see her drinking and smoking pot and cigarettes. A few minutes after the joint made the rounds, she began giggling and couldn't stop.

I kinda wished I hadn't come. This was making me nervous. If I returned home smelling like pot or even cigarettes, I couldn't even imagine how much trouble I'd be in. Right now I was being punished for almost nothing. What would marijuana and beer get me?

"Oh, shit," James sat bolt upright and stared out the windshield. Then he turned the ignition key, but the car didn't start.

I looked over the front seat to see a pair of headlights coming at us.

James hit the ignition again. Nothing. Suddenly, we were blinded by a searchlight attached to the car that was moving in our direction. James's and Mandy's heads were silhouettes.

"Cop," James said.

I'd worried about returning home smelling like smoke, but I'd never thought of something like this. A cop arresting us for marijuana and underage drinking. My life was over. I should just kill myself right now. Cop in front of us. Dead end road. Beer and pot. No way out.

"Toss the beer!" Noel shouted as James continued his struggle to start the car. We rolled down windows, tossing opened and unopened cans.

The ignition caught and the engine rumbled to life. I could feel it under my feet. As I watched in disbelief, James put the car in gear and tromped the accelerator. Keeping the headlights off, he shot to one side of the narrow road. I could have touched the cop car as we flew past, and I saw the officer behind the wheel. We fishtailed away. I looked over my shoulder. Enveloped in a cloud of dust, the cop hit the dead end and turned his car in the tight space, losing precious time. As he maneuvered, he shined the spotlight on the beer cans littering the ground. Evidence.

"Here!" Noel shoved something in my hand. A joint. "Eat it," he said.

He passed the remaining joints around, and the four of us began shoving them in our mouths. I choked and gagged and chewed as the joint expanded.

"Don't chew it!" Noel said, when he realized what I was doing. Too late.

"I never took a class on joint swallowing," I said, my mouth full. I finally got it down, but I probably had enough pot left in my teeth to get arrested.

The cop was behind us now, siren and red light going.

James took a quick left, then a right, then another left, and suddenly we were in a residential area. I didn't know if it was just luck, or if he'd been here before.

"I can't believe you're doing this!" I shouted, one hand gripping the back of his seat. The roar of the engine made it hard to hear my own voice. Tires squealed as we turned corners. The car bottomed out, sparks flying. I went airborne, my head hitting the ceiling. Mandy was giggling even harder now.

"If he catches me I'll go to prison," James said.

I tried to reason with him. "You can't outrun a cop. You're going to be in more trouble now."

He ignored me. We whipped around a corner, flew down a tangled maze of suburban streets. I hoped he wouldn't hit anyone, like some little kid riding his tricycle. But it was late. Kids were in bed. Okay, some innocent adult out walking his dog.

"I think maybe we lost him," Noel said.

Everything was moving fast. I could hear the siren, but could no longer see the lights.

Another sharp turn, the squeal of brakes. We came to an abrupt halt and James cut the engine. We were parked in a driveway, in front of a two-car garage that belonged to a ranch-style home. A nice upper-class place.

"Get down," James whispered loudly.

All four of us hit the floor.

"That was some amazing driving," Noel whispered, his face inches from mine, his voice full of awe. I would need more time to fully grasp what had just happened.

In the dark, James said, "I don't think he got a good look at the car, and I doubt he had time to get the plate number."

I heard the siren coming closer and saw the glare of headlights above my head. We were dead. Dead, dead, dead.

The police car slowed … then moved down the street. The cop shut off the siren.

"He's gone," Mandy said.

"Stay down," James said. "He wants us to think he's left."

He was right. The police car returned, this time moving silently through the streets, headlights off. He knew we were here, but James had been right. He didn't recognize the car.

He passed us four times. We waited another fifteen minutes before James slowly sat up and looked around. Then he started the car, backed out of the driveway, and drove off.

"Do you think he's called other cops?" I asked.

"Maybe," James said. "Maybe not. If I'd lost the car I was tailing, I don't know if I'd want the whole force to know about it."

"Let's get out of here," I said. "Let's get out of town."

"No, let's go the to movie like we planned," Noel said. "A crowded parking lot. We'll get away from the car, watch the movie, and see if there are any cops around when we come back out."

"A theater will be the best place to hide," James agreed.

How could they think of going to a movie now? "You people are insane," I said.

Mandy giggled. "That was so funny."

My heart slammed in my chest as we moved slowly through town, obeying speed limits, not racing through yellow lights. The theater was packed, and it was hard to find a place to park. We got out of the car, and I felt exposed. The lot was brightly lit.

Once inside, I felt a little better. Nobody could tie me to anything.

I couldn't concentrate on the movie. I kept waiting to feel stoned from the giant joint I'd swallowed, but I think I had too much adrenalin racing through my body. I kept replaying our great escape. I'd never been around somebody who could think and react so quickly. I kept waiting for the cops to come, waiting for them to walk up and down the aisle with flashlights, or even stop the movie and turn on the overhead lights. It didn't happen.

I wouldn't have been able to tell anybody what the movie was about. I hoped I didn't get quizzed once I returned home. They would think I hadn't really gone. At one point, I went to the restroom and looked in the mirror. My teeth were full of green chunks of marijuana. I hand-cupped water to my mouth, rinsed, and spit, washing the evidence down the drain.

The movie credits finally rolled, but I was nervous about heading outside. Would cops be watching and waiting for us?

"I don't want to go back to the car," I said.

"Let's just head that way," Noel said. "We'll walk past the car to see if any cops are watching."

We did. And saw nothing. But someone could have been in an unmarked vehicle. I couldn't believe we'd been able to get away from them. It didn't seem possible. Kids outrunning and outsmarting cops.

We roamed around the lot for a couple of minutes, acting as if we were searching for our vehicle.

"Let's leave with the mob," Noel said. "We don't want to be the last ones here."

We dove in the car and joined the line of theatergoers waiting to exit. My heart was pounding again. I wanted to hurry, I wanted James to gun it and get us out of there, but that would have been stupid.

Finally we exited the lot and headed south on Main Street, in the direction of Artesia. Once we were out of town, I kept looking over my shoulder.

I tried to imagine the cop who'd lost us. What was he thinking? What was he doing? Did he tell anybody? I remembered the surprise on his face as we'd roared past him.

We began to laugh. We relived the events, beginning with the arrival of the cop on the dirt road. Everybody had noticed something different. We laughed about how the spotlight had lit up the beer cans. We laughed about my trying to eat the joint. I told them about my teeth, and we laughed some more.

We talked about James's driving. His incredible driving.

The house. Why hadn't anybody come out of the house? Crazy luck.

"That was the most insane thing I've ever experienced," I said. And that was saying a lot when I thought about the string of mental cases my mother had dated over the years.

Later, Noel walked me to the door of my house. The porch light was on, but it was dark inside. "I'm sorry about tonight," Noel said. "Do you think you'll ever want to go out with me again?" He had a weird look in his eyes that made me feel uncomfortable. It reminded me of the desperation I sometimes saw in David's face. But no, I must have imagined it.

"Do you ever do anything like just go bowling?" I asked.

"How about playing pinball?"

"I love pinball."

He didn't try to kiss me. Thank God, he didn't try to kiss me.

Before going inside, I removed my shoes and quietly turned the doorknob. I locked the door behind me and tiptoed down the dark hallway. I was hungry, but I didn't dare open the refrigerator or turn on a faucet to get a drink. Holding my breath, I slipped into my room and shut the door. I stood there in the dark and listened and waited.

I heard muffled voices. I heard a creak, then silence. Beautiful silence. I shed my clothes, put on a nightshirt, crawled into bed, and pulled the covers to my chin.

This had been the most incredible night ever.

Yes, we broke the law. But I'd learned something valuable. Adults didn't always win. And more incredible, I'd finally done something worthy of punishment and hadn't gotten caught. David and my mother were sleeping across the hall, oblivious to what had taken place a few hours ago. I felt an odd sense of power.

Chapter 18

The role of a housewife provided too much time to think, to dwell on the past and the present. My mother's eyes often looked strange, all pupil and glassy. I'd seen that glassiness before, just for a few minutes, or maybe an hour, but now her eyes looked weird most of the time. Did she drink when we were away at school? I didn't think so. She never smelled like booze. But what did she do all day? Alone with her thoughts?

She had a habit of writing long letters to people who'd done her wrong. Did she spend her days in the tiny dark house writing letters to my dad? Did she *call* him? Rage at him over the telephone? These things wouldn't have surprised me.

Was she simply depressed about her new marriage, or was something more serious going on? I could follow a backwards path and see that each traumatic or stressful event in her life had carried her deeper into what I called her mental decay. Had her marriage sent her over the edge?

She'd spent the past seven years trying to find a new husband. Now she had one, and I'd never seen her so miserable. Not a flicker of happiness there. Just a dark hole. But maybe it wasn't about my dad or about David.

Maybe men weren't good for her. Maybe men weren't good for any woman.

In our new life, my mother put on a show, an act for any strangers who might happen by. She billed herself as the vivacious artist, the talented chef, the beautiful woman who'd married a teacher. But nobody really knew her. Who was she? Who had she ever been?

It always went back to my dad. Sometimes I thought she was over him. She lived in a place that was nothing like Florida. She was married to an academic, not someone who spent his days on the ocean. So different. But she couldn't run far enough. She needed a machine, something that would erase all memories of him, of that other man, the one who'd betrayed her. I think if she'd been able to get him out of her head, maybe she would have been okay. Maybe she would have been happy.

But the decay was there, deep and bitter. There was no getting rid of it. She would never be happy again. There might be moments. Small rewards that brought pleasure, but true happiness seemed forever beyond her grasp. And maybe deep down she knew it.

*

Weeks after the move to Artesia, the old wedding album appeared. One day I arrived home from school and entered the house with typical caution, the way I always did, hoping to make it to the bedroom without doing anything to annoy my mother or draw attention to myself. But when I spotted the album on the couch, I stopped and stared. It had yellowed over the years, and my mind jumped from location to location, going through all of our different lives, seeing it on the dining room table in Florida, then Burlington, then Albuquerque.

Now, years later, it still held a promise of another life, a better life. Like a remembered scent, seeing the album brought back old feelings with startling immediacy. Maybe it represented where we began, and what we'd once been. It reached from the past, from Florida and Iowa, to reassure me. This is where we came from. This place where things were once okay. And if they'd been okay before, maybe they could be okay again. Even though I was older, I experienced the same hope I'd felt as a little kid. The waiting for my father to come back.

"What is that doing out?" I asked.

My mother hovered in the kitchen, in front of the teakettle. She shut off the gas flame and poured hot water into a clay mug. Grasping it with both hands, she walked to the couch and looked down at the album. "I'm trying to decide what to do with it," she said. Her hair was almost shoulder-length, dark, straight. She wore jeans and a chambray work shirt, the sleeves rolled a few turns. On her wrist was a wide silver bracelet. I could smell the tea in her cup, something woodsy and dark.

I thought of responses, weighing each one in my head, trying to find the most harmless, the one the least likely to set her off. She seemed calm today, the tone of her voice smooth, normal. I liked her this way. This was the way I always wanted to think of her. A mug in her hands, her body relaxed.

I didn't say anything. I couldn't find harmless words.

I wanted to pick up the album the way I used to. I wanted to open it to the first page. If she opened it, okay. Otherwise, I wouldn't touch it.

I heard a movement in the hall. "Here comes the bride!" my brother shouted.

He hadn't gone to school. My mother kept him home a lot, I think because she couldn't stand to be alone. The two of them played, and when David returned from work they never mentioned that Jude hadn't left the house that day.

I heard the sound of rustling fabric, and my brother appeared in the hallway wearing my mother's white wedding gown. He was only seven, so most of it was bunched under his arms, a big cloud that surrounded him.

I held my breath. What would she say? What would she do? My brother could get away with a lot, but this . . .

She laughed. So much that she grew weak and dropped on the couch. Tears ran down her cheeks.

Jude played it up. He swooped around the room, he twirled.

"Wait. I have to get the camera," our mother said. She dashed to the bedroom.

"I can't believe you put on her wedding dress," I whispered to my brother.

His brows went up, and he made a surprised face, as if reenacting an earlier reaction. "It wasn't my idea."

There was no time to ask more. Our mother returned with camera in hand. She had him pose, and she took frame after frame. "I can't wait to get these developed," she said. "Wouldn't that be hilarious if I sent copies to *him*?"

No doubt who she was talking about.

"I'll get them enlarged. I'll send him and that pig copies."

Maybe this wasn't so weird. Maybe it was just silly fun. Maybe this was her way of moving on. She couldn't really care anymore if she was doing such silly things to a sacred object.

A car pulled up outside.

"Hurry!" she whispered to Jude. "Go take it off! Hide it!"

In a rustle of fabric, he tripped and stumbled and laughed his way to the bedroom while Mom hid the wedding album under the couch.

David came in the front door, briefcase in his hand. He and my mother kissed like two people on television. Her face was still flushed.

"Taking pictures?" he asked, spotting the camera in her hand. Oblivious. If he knew her, really knew her, he'd know something was going on. And yet he didn't see any difference in her from day to day. He couldn't tell when she was sad or when she was happy. Or when she needed to hear that she had a problem. He couldn't tell when she wanted nothing more than to chop us into tiny pieces and bury us in the backyard, or when she was so blissfully happy she might put on her old wedding gown and drive to the A&W just to be outrageous.

I felt sorry for him again. My emotions confused me, because I wanted to hate him. I wasn't sure he deserved my sympathy. And sympathy toward him, toward either of them, was a weakness.

Chapter 19

Fifteen minutes after the wedding-dress incident, I decided to squeeze in an hour of tanning before the sun got too low. I put on my yellow and blue bikini and spread a towel on the cement patio in the backyard.

I loved to sunbathe. Something about closing my eyes and letting myself bake. The scent of baby oil and iodine, the muffled sounds of the world, took the form of meditation.

I hadn't been outside long when I heard a movement at the backdoor. I shielded my eyes with my hand to see David standing in the opening.

"You look like one of those girls in a magazine," he said. "Like a model." He was staring at me with surprise and admiration, naively voicing a thought he should have kept to himself. I was just a kid, but I could see that he didn't know how to interact with other people. I suppose being raised by monks or Brothers or whatever they were might mess up a person in a big way. His childhood made mine seem normal.

My experience with the opposite sex was a single kiss from a boy with lips so soft they'd made me dizzy, and I wasn't used to men or boys looking at me the way David was looking at me. His comment conveyed a sense of ownership that made me uncomfortable, yet at the same time he had this goofy, pleased expression on his face, as if he'd just discovered some pretty flower he wanted to pick and show to Mommy.

I grabbed the big shirt I used for a cover-up and waited for him to leave, but he remained in the doorway.

From the darkness of the house, my mother appeared behind him. "What's going on out here? What are you two doing?"

"I just said she looks like somebody in a magazine. Doesn't she look like a girl in a magazine?"

Stupid man. He was grinning, pleased with himself, expecting my mother to pat him on the head, oblivious to the storm standing at his elbow. It amazed me that he couldn't read her moods.

She shrieked and swung her fist at him. "Don't say that! Don't look at her!" Then to me, "Get dressed! Get in the house! Go to your room. Now!"

They both vanished.

I scrambled to my feet and slipped into the shirt, buttoned two buttons, grabbed the towel and wrapped it around my waist. Inside, I followed the sounds of screaming and sobbing to see David outside their closed bedroom door, one tentative hand against the wood, as he whispered in the crack, "Come on, hon. Let me in. Unlock the door."

"Get away!" she shouted from the other side.

I squeezed past him to reach my room, but he seemed unaware of me, all of his focus on his angry wife.

"Please, Nan," he said, mouth to the crack. "Please. I'm sorry. I'll never do that again. I'll never say that again. I'll never look at her again. Unlock the door." He whimpered. "Please."

The sobs continued.

How could she have thought he was attracted to me? But maybe that wasn't why she was upset. I examined the event from another angle. Men had always found her beautiful and sexy, but she was getting older, heavier. Had she married him because she didn't think she'd find anybody else? How disturbing to find the man you just married drooling over your daughter. But she was the one who'd turned it into something it wasn't. She didn't seem to know him any better than he knew her.

In my room, I slipped a pair of cutoffs over my bikini bottoms and finished buttoning the cover-up.

Through my closed door, I heard David trying to coax her from the room. "I'm going to get a screwdriver and remove the handle if you don't unlock the door," he said.

"Don't you dare!" she responded. "If you remove the handle, I'll divorce you. Do you hear me?"

He let out a fresh whimper and didn't leave his post.

An hour later, I heard the click of a latch and the squeak of a door hinge, then the sound of low conversation as he tried to soothe her. Another hour passed and they exited the bedroom. That was followed by sounds of silverware coming from the kitchen, dinner being prepared.

I left my room. My little brother's door was open. He sat inside, playing with a model airplane, ignoring the drama.

In the kitchen, my mother faced the stove while David sat at the kitchen table reading a newspaper as if nothing had happened. That's how this worked.

"Need any help?" I asked. Everything we did, everything we said, was about appeasing her.

My mother swung around, a wooden spoon in her hand. "Don't talk to me. Do you understand? You aren't anything to me."

Nothing she said or did make any sense.

"I'm sorry. I won't sunbathe anymore. I didn't know it would be a big deal." They were acting as if I'd been naked. My bikini bottoms almost covered my belly button. I'd never even thought of the outfit as sexy. I'd just wanted to lie in the sun.

The spoon came at me. I raised an arm and managed to dodge the strike. I wasn't sure what she was cooking, but something hit the floor. It looked like chili.

David was still hiding behind the paper. I wanted him to do something. I wanted him to take charge. To help her. *Help us.*

With a crinkle of paper, he turned the page and vanished again. Coward. It occurred to me that he and my father had one big thing in common: neither would ever do anything heroic, and mothers and fathers should be heroes.

Up until now, I'd hoped some shred of a decent human might emerge from David, but that was never going to happen. He couldn't be depended upon to set this straight, to take charge.

I cleared my throat and stood a little straighter. "I hate to say this, but you need help."

Eyes red-rimmed from crying cut a hole right through me. "What are you talking about?" Her voice was low, telling me I'd better backtrack or things would get bad fast. David's paper quit rustling. He lowered it a few inches. Watching. Listening. Doing nothing.

"You need help." I tried to keep my voice level. Tried to sound practical. Adult. "Like a doctor's help."

"Are you saying what I think you're saying?" Her eyes shimmered.

The paper was down all the way now as David watched from behind thick glasses.

"I think you need a psychiatrist," I said. "I think maybe you need medication."

The word medication did it. It wasn't like pulling the pin from a grenade, because a grenade gave you a couple of seconds. This was instant. I saw murder in her eyes.

I turned.

I could outrun her. I could outrun them both. To my room. I would slam the door. Lock it. Wait for her to cool off. Again.

My bare feet flew down the hallway. When I reached my brother's room, a hand shot out. It grabbed me by the ankle, tripping me. I hit the floor. Just as quickly, I rebounded, but the fall had cost me precious seconds. My brother stared at me, a look of smug satisfaction on his face.

He was one of them now.

They were right behind me. In the bedroom, I fumbled for the lock. The door flew open, slamming against the wall.

Together, they took me down. Fists pummeled my head, feet kicked my stomach. An extension cord materialized, and the pronged end bit into my thighs and cut my arms as I tried to shield myself.

"Hold her! Hold her!" My mother shrieked and sobbed at the same time. "Hit her. Hit her! Harder! Harder!" Clawed hands ripped at my hair. My head was slammed against the floor again and again. I tasted blood. I began to wonder if this was it. If I would die. They were stronger than I was. Much stronger, and they had white-hot crazy rage on their side.

I hoped they killed me. I hoped they killed me and I hoped they both went to prison for life. Did New Mexico have the death penalty?

"You're insane!" I shouted. At last I was finally able to speak my mind because I had no fear; nothing could get worse. "Insane! Can't you see that, David? You need to do something. You need to make her go to a doctor!"

Just an hour ago, the three of us, mother and children, had laughed together.

The word insane recharged her. With a fresh wave of strength, she beat my head against the floor while David held me down.

I think it might have gone on forever if they hadn't worn themselves out. When the beating finally stopped, I remained curled on the floor, waiting for more blows. Both of them straightened, breathing hard, faces flushed. David bent and picked up his glasses, which had been knocked from his face in the struggle. He tried to put them on, but they were broken. Good.

My mother was sobbing hysterically. "You aren't related to me," she said. "You are nothing to me. *Nothing*! You are nothing but a boarder here. We will keep a roof over your head, but the next time you say anything like that, you're not coming back in this house. Do you hear me? I will lock the door and you will never step inside again!"

David put his arm around her, making comforting sounds. Together, they left.

I lay on the floor for a long time, wondering if anything was broken. I hurt all over. My scalp, my face, my stomach, my arms and legs where the cord had hit.

Had I stepped over the line? A kid telling her mother she was crazy? Maybe it *was* my fault. Maybe I'd asked for it. No. I couldn't start thinking like that.

My little brother.

I was surprised but not surprised. This new life was all about survival, and he was doing what he could to avoid a beating. By tripping me, he'd shown them whose side he was on; he'd shown them that they could trust him. He wanted to make sure he never received the same kind of punishment. He'd signed the paper; he'd agreed to be a part of their insanity.

I crawled into bed, hoping I would die in my sleep. But that kind of thing only happened in the movies. When I woke up the next morning, my face was swollen, my stomach and legs were covered in cuts and bruises, and I had a bald spot on my head.

And I had to go to school.

These are the things we hide. I don't know why. It wasn't my shame, it was theirs. But it wasn't about the pain, it was about the humiliation. The pain was nothing. But I couldn't be humiliated if nobody knew about it.

I put makeup on my face, and wore a long prairie skirt that fell to the floor. Over the peasant top, I gingerly slipped on a sweater to cover the bruises on my arms. Eyeliner and mascara and eye shadow. Yes, I was hiding.

Without glancing at my brother—I wasn't sure I could ever think of him in the same way after last night—I left the house.

I should run away, hitchhike from Artesia. How? I had no money. Where would I go? I had to have a plan. I had to think it out. And my cat. I couldn't leave my cat with them.

I would return to the house on Juniper Street once school was over for the day. I would try to figure out what to do.

Chapter 20

I'd planned to stay away until dark. I figured the less time I spent at home the better, but I got hungry. I'd almost expected to find the front door locked, but the knob turned and the door opened. In the kitchen I made a sandwich, poured a glass of orange juice, and headed down the hall to my room, closing the door behind me.

The cat food I'd put out that morning hadn't been disturbed.

"Ying?"

I looked under the bed. I looked in the closet.

Had they gotten rid of him? It had happened before with other animals. My mother would get us pets when she was happy, and get rid of them when she was sad.

Or had they thrown him outside? I went to the backdoor and called his name. Nothing. I finally found him in the garage, hiding behind some boxes. His body was limp, his eyes glazed.

I found David and my mother sitting on the couch watching the news, black & white protest footage. David's arm was around her shoulders. I hadn't planned to ever talk to either of them again, but now I had to.

"Ying is sick," I said. "He needs to go to the vet."

A look passed between them. My mother finally said, "Who's going to pay for a vet? You don't have any money and we can't afford it."

I was trying to read her, trying to see if the two of them had somehow been behind my cat's illness. I pictured her kicking him across the room. I pictured David hitting him with the car, maybe not even knowing it.

"I'll pay you back with the money I make watching Estelle."

They both went to the garage. After a few minutes they decided David would drive me to the vet. The lack of argument made me suspicious again. Had they already known the cat was injured?

But at the veterinarian's office, we found out Ying had kidney disease.

"I'm sorry, the prognosis isn't good," the vet said. "We can operate, but it probably won't save him. I would suggest you have him put down."

I began crying hysterically.

"Let's take him home and talk about it," David said.

Numbly, I followed him out to the car carrying the cardboard box with my cat inside.

"He needs to be put down," David said, explaining the situation to my mother. "The surgery doesn't sound as if it will be effective."

I could now see how much the cat was suffering, and I wished we hadn't brought him home. He was in pain. His pupils were solid black, and glazed, and occasionally he let out an awful cry. "Let's go back," I said. "I want to have him put to sleep."

David checked his watch. "The vet is probably closed now. And anyway, euthanasia isn't cheap. Seems a waste of good money to pay a vet to kill a cat."

"I agree," my mother said.

"But he's suffering!" I hated to think of waiting all night, but now it didn't sound as if they would even take me to the vet in the morning. How could I get him there? How could I pay? Would they need the money right away, or would they bill me so I could pay later?

David left for the garage, and returned carrying a baseball bat. "I'll hit him in the head and that will be that. One blow and he'll be dead. It's called a rabbit punch."

I couldn't believe what I was hearing. "Ying isn't a rabbit! Let me take him to the vet in the morning." I was crying. "You can't beat him with a bat."

"It will just be a punch," David said. "I'll do it in the desert so you don't have to hear it."

"I want to take him to the vet!"

"No," my mother said. "David will take him to the desert."

David reappeared holding a flashlight.

"What will you do with him after he's dead?" This couldn't be happening.

David picked up the box. Ying let out a yowl. I imagined David driving down the highway, tossing the box out the window. I imagined him beating my cat in the head, and poor Ying trying to crawl away while David continued to strike him with the bat.

"No!" I was hysterical. "You can't take him! You can't do this!"

"I've already put a shovel in the car. I'll bury him where I kill him. It will be easy."

Now I imagined him tossing him in a hole and burying him alive. "No!"

I grabbed the box and tried to make a run for it. David wrenched it from my hands, and I let it go because Ying was yowling in pain.

David left with the box under his arm.

"It's the best thing to do," my mother said. "We'll be saving money, and the problem will be dealt with tonight rather than in the morning."

I remembered the pets she'd gotten rid of in the past. Usually when we were away at school, or visiting our grandmother. Our father. Now I wondered if she'd bludgeoned any of them to death.

He would suffer. I knew he would suffer.

But maybe he was too far-gone to feel much more pain. I had to cling to that hope. That he was already close to death. So close that one poorly aimed tap would kill him. Yes, I had to hope for that. Hope, hope, hope.

I'd heard about a man in Wisconsin who made lampshades out of human skin and even ate people.

This was like that. That kind of sick-in-the-belly disbelief that these people existed. And that they did these horrible things without any thought that maybe this was wrong. My mother wasn't right, but David wasn't right either. Killing my cat had been his idea, not my mother's. And the way he would carry it out. Not with a gun. A gun would have been better, but then, knowing David, he would have missed. But the idea of bashing a sick animal in the head . . .

Chapter 21

My life in the little desert town became an accepted prison sentence, but that didn't stop me from mentally counting the months and years until it would end, until I could pack my things and walk away from the cult of two. At school, teachers wanted to know if I was okay. My gym teacher asked about the bruises on the backs of my thighs, new ones appearing before the old ones healed.

"If you're having problems at home," my science teacher, Mr. Bodin, said, catching me as I was leaving his classroom, "you should think about finding an adult to talk to. A relative. A friend, even a teacher." Mr. Bodin was a football coach, and I was touched and surprised that he would take the time to worry about me.

I didn't want to lie, but I had no choice. My life would be ten times as horrible if I said anything. And I also felt a strange need to keep up a façade, and even a need to protect my mother and David. They seemed, in some ways, like children. "Everything is okay."

He knew I wasn't telling the truth, but he didn't seem mad. Instead, his face held a compassion that made me want to spill everything. I'd always sensed that he saw potential in me, and his slight encouragements made me want to push myself. He was one of the few people who saw past my act as the class clown. "Remember what I said," he told me.

I nodded because I couldn't speak. My throat was tight, and my eyes burned. I ducked my head, clutched my books to my chest, and hurried from the room.

Chapter 22

Noel was my escape. I was allowed to go anywhere with him. School functions, even parties. It didn't matter. If he pulled up to my house, I could go. He was my Get-Out-of-Jail-Free card. With him, I had a life outside the walls of my home, a life that was tied to school and tied to friends. And as school relationships became stronger, the things that went on inside my home became less significant. I could tolerate them as long as I escaped to places like school, and even Julie's house.

I was leading two lives, the secret life that took place behind the walls of our tiny house, the life with the miserable woman who'd married the wrong man, and my school life.

I was one of the funniest kids in my class, but not at home. Never at home. The few friends who visited my house never returned. My mother scared them away, and David gave them the creeps.

Sometimes I wished Thomas lived with us. My younger brother was too little to get it, he was too happy to finally have a father, and there was none of the weird stuff going on with him. Thomas would have confirmed that David and my mother weren't right, and that I wasn't a bad kid or hadn't lost my mind.

In the dead of night, when I couldn't sleep, lying in the darkness, feeling unsafe knowing they were a few feet away, I tried to figure it out, tried to understand what had happened and why. My brain wanted to make sense of it.

How could a mother not love her own children? That was the puzzle. We weren't ugly and malformed. We weren't stupid. We weren't evil.

But we'd all been what my mother called accidents. She was a devout Catholic and hadn't used birth control. Even her marriage to David had been driven by religion. My being allowed to hang out with Noel was because he was a Catholic. If religion were removed from our lives, what would remain? Would she have gotten herself into this mess? Would she have had kids at all? Or would she have had abortions? And another question: Why hadn't she given us up for adoption? Had she thought about it?

The unhappier she was, the more pain she needed to cause. I don't know what it did for her, what she got out of it, but she looked for small misdeeds to justify her behavior. Forgetting to put a dirty spoon in the special cup just for dirty silverware. Missing a spot of dust on the living room table. These were things that gave her a reason to punish me because she needed to cause pain, physical and mental.

My mother was gone. I didn't know the person who now inhabited her skin, but it wasn't my mother. And the world inside our house was not me. I had to somehow live there, eat there, and sleep there, without allowing it to touch the person I was deep inside.

And so I learned how to shut myself off when I stepped in the door. I learned to not care and not feel, and to exist in a semi-conscious way within those walls. I would talk to David and my mother when needed, but I hid inside myself, watching them from behind my eyes, not through my eyes.

My little brother had an Instamatic camera, and he snapped a few photos of me. Pictures of the walking dead. Me, comatose, but standing upright. A blank, expressionless face, because emotions got me in trouble. The sound of laughter, a smile, these were things that set her off, that infuriated her. She couldn't stand to see a smile on anyone's face. How odd, to not want your own child to be happy.

If I ever had kids, I'd be crazy about them. I would listen to them, I would talk to them, I would be the one they came to if they had a problem. I would love them.

Chapter 23

I stepped out of Julie's house. I'd been going there every Thursday for six months, but tonight was my last night. Tonight I'd kissed Estelle's soft cheek one last time because she and Julie were moving away to New Orleans, where Estelle would be put in a nursing home and Julie would pick up the threads of her old life. It was all so sad.

Noel's car waited at the end of the sidewalk, under the streetlight. Once I was in the passenger seat, he headed in the direction of home, oddly silent as he pulled up to my door. I didn't like this kind of silence. In my house, the silence of others never ended well. This was the kind of silence that came before words I didn't want to hear.

Even though it was late, lights were on inside. Another bad sign.

Noel turned off the radio and turned off the car engine. "I have to tell you something." He sounded nervous, and I heard him swallow. I wanted to leave. I wanted to run.

I glanced at the living-room window. The curtains were closed, but I could see the outline of a lamp. Behind it, a shadow of movement. This was the worst part of the day, the most frightening, opening the door to my own house, not knowing what I would find inside.

Did Noel want to kiss me? I hoped not. So far, he'd never as much as tried to hold my hand, and I'd begun to think that this was our relationship. Friends. That was more than fine with me. But what happened next took me completely by surprise.

"I love you," he blurted out.

Not what I expected. Not, not, not what I expected. I gasped and looked away.

"I love you," he repeated, when I didn't respond.

My vision darkened, and I heard a whooshing, like a shell being held to my ear. How many times had I done that when we lived in Florida? Gone to the beach and put a shell to my ear? It had never sounded like the ocean to me, but voices. Whispers from some other place. And now it almost seemed I was on the receiving end of some magic phone call from the past, and those whispers from those shells had tried to warn me of this life and this moment.

"Maybe it's dolphins talking underwater," my father had said.

And I remembered him there, not on the beach, but in our house. He'd brought a huge pink conch shell home for me.

"I think it's mermaids," I'd told him. "Mermaids calling to their children."

He'd played along. "What are they saying?"

"Come home, lost babies."

Now I imagined my father at the other end of a shell conversation, and I said, "Come and get me. Come and take me away from this place."

"You don't love me," I told Noel. I stared straight ahead, through the windshield. I couldn't look at him. How awful of me to have gone out with him to begin with. But I'd never guessed he'd fall in love with someone who didn't exist. Yet I couldn't help but feel that I'd tricked him. I'd created this person just for him, the person who wasn't me.

"I *do* love you," he insisted. "I can't imagine living without you."

I turned my head. He was staring at me in the very way I'd seen David look at my mother, with a kind of sick yearning. Lovesick. And I suddenly saw him in a different way, not as Noel, my friend, but as a threat. As someone else who was out to hurt me. And in some way, I resented his confession. I couldn't deal with it, not on top of everything else.

I wanted to scream. I wanted to act like my mother. "You're seventeen," I reminded him, trying not to freak out. A seventeen-year-old didn't know about love. From what I could tell, adults didn't know about love.

"Eighteen in a few weeks," he reminded me. "I'll be going to college soon."

"The person you think you love doesn't exist." I couldn't tell him that I'd invented her to tolerate this new, intolerable life. He was in love with a funny, happy girl, not me. Not this dark person, this hurting person who had never shared any of my real life with him. I didn't want him to know about the person I became when I stepped inside my house. I needed him to believe in the girl I wasn't. The strong girl.

He grabbed my arms and leaned close. I shrugged him off, shook him off.

My response confused him.

What a mistake I'd made. What an awful mistake. I'd led him on. I hadn't meant to. I hadn't understood what was happening. I'd never dreamed that he'd like me that way. This was all wrong. Horribly wrong. I could never be held and kissed and owned, not even by Noel. Especially by Noel. In some twisted part of my brain, I imagined this kind of ownership happening with someone else, maybe someone I didn't care about. Then maybe I could do it. Why did that seem right? And this seem wrong? How did that make sense? How did that make any sense? But it did.

"I can't see you again." Terrified, I jumped from the car and slammed the door.

I didn't want to look at him, but I couldn't help myself. The streetlamp was a spotlight on his face. He was crying. *Crying.* He was looking at me as if I'd just broken his heart. *Would you like to try to break my heart?*

I ran, and it took me a year to get from his car to my front door even though it wasn't far at all. The entire world had stopped except for me. Like I was running through a still photograph. At the same time, everything seemed more defined. The weird raised area near the curb where I stumbled and almost fell. The sidewalk with cracks I could feel through the soles of my sandals. The cold metal of the column that held up the front porch. The smell of the town, of the oil refinery that I'd gotten so used to I often forgot it was there at the end of Main Street. All of these things meshed with the feeling of Noel's eyes on my back, and the hurt that was radiating from inside his car. I'd never in my life ever hurt anybody. It was unbearable.

I slipped into the house. Inside was as bad as outside. That's what I knew as soon as I closed the door behind me, but I'd known it when I'd seen the lights.

My mother's eyes had that glazed, glassy look, and I knew she'd been waiting for me. From outside, I heard Noel's car pull away. What was he thinking? How much had I hurt him?

How long would he hurt? Hours? Days? Weeks? No, surely not weeks.

Returning my focus to my mother, I ran down the list of things I might have done or not done. A glass not rinsed and put in the dishwasher. A towel left on the bathroom floor.

"I was in your room today." She held up a stack of letters I'd received from my friend in Albuquerque. "I read these. Every one of them."

I couldn't imagine how boring the letters must have been. Teenager talk of music and the cute new boy at school.

"You can't have any contact with Robin again. And you are grounded for the next two months."

"Why?"

"Do you have to ask?" She shook the letters at me. "Filth. Nasty, nasty filth."

"I don't know what you're talking about." Robin didn't cuss. She didn't do drugs. She didn't drink. She didn't have sex.

"She called her period the curse. The curse."

I hadn't reacted to my mother's lack of logic for a long time, but now I laughed. She'd hoped to find something big, something bad, but this was all she could come up with. The curse.

"From now on, when letters from her arrive, I'll return them. You will have no more contact with her. Ever. Do you understand? You can't write to her, and she can't write to you."

Anything that gave me the smallest pleasure was taken away. And I wondered if she was disturbed by the letters with the Albuquerque postmark that arrived in the mailbox two or three times a week.

Maybe she couldn't bear the constant reminders of the life we'd left behind.

I waited for her to hit me for laughing, but it didn't happen. That might come later. That punishment might be delivered by David. But just a few days ago she'd commented on the bruises on the backs of my legs. Maybe she was trying to restrain herself.

That night, I wrote a letter to my father. I hadn't had any contact with him in years, not since our trip to California, and I wasn't even sure he lived in the same place, the house where Jude had pushed the girl in the pool. Those days had seemed so dark when they were happening, but now, looking back, they seemed wonderful, even the trip to the pizza parlor where Eve had chewed out the waitress seemed like light fun in comparison to this life. And even Eve seemed more foolish than evil.

In my letter, I hinted that I was unhappy. I told him about the town where we lived, and told him about school and the classes I liked—literature and science and art. If he replied, I might tell him more. About David. About my mother. About how she needed to see a doctor. And about my dreams of becoming an artist.

I thought a moment, then signed the letter *Love, Theresa*, and included my address and phone number. On a plain sheet of paper, I drew a shell, hoping he might remember the shells he'd brought home to me, then I folded both sheets several times and stuck them in a small envelope. I couldn't mail the letter from home. I would drop it in a mailbox tomorrow.

Would he answer? Would he write back? Would he call? No, but I'd wait anyway.

*

Noel was heartbroken when I ran from him, but he quickly learned to hate me. When we passed in the school hallway he looked right through me as if I didn't exist.

All for the best. Hate was easier than love.

But sometimes I'd catch him staring at me from across the room, trying to figure it all out. Maybe he would get it if I told him everything. About my mother. About David. Even then, I didn't think he'd understand. He'd loved someone who didn't exist. He'd loved the person I wanted to be, not the person I was. So I let it go. I said nothing. And those few times when I caught him looking at me, he would glance away, but not before I saw the pain in his eyes.

I hoped that someday he would talk to me again. I hoped that someday we would be friends…

And then he graduated and was gone.

Chapter 24

I don't remember where the rumors started. Maybe in class. Maybe at home. Maybe at the hamburger and taco joint across from the high school. Talk about the college closing. I'd noticed a change in David. Now when he arrived home, he didn't stride in the door with his head high, proud of his job, proud of his wife. His shoulders were hunched, as if the briefcase he carried was too heavy. He'd drop it on the couch and follow it down like a dead body following a cement block. Then he would sit and stare blankly at a television that blared footage of the Vietnam War—the soundtrack of our lives.

"Is the college closing?" Jude asked one night at the dinner table. "People at school said it is."

The College of Artesia was based on something called the Parsons Plan, and other Parsons colleges around the country had folded. There had been accusations of falsified grades for draft dodgers, and accreditation was pulled. But David told us that wouldn't happen in Artesia because no grades had been falsified.

"The town won't let the college close," David assured us, even though his body language said something else. "They'll approve a tax levy that will keep us going."

"People in town hate the college," I told him. He didn't understand. He didn't hear the way residents talked about it. The pretend school. The school for draft dodgers. And a bigger complaint: the college was corrupting the kids. Along with a questionable education, it had brought sex, drugs, and rock and roll to town.

"It doesn't make good business sense to close it," David said. "The college *is* the town."

But one day we were being assured that everything was fine; the next it was over and no amount of denial could change the course of events. The town voted down an increase in taxes, and it was announced that the school would close at the end of the spring semester.

Two years and a few months. That's how long we'd been there.

Overnight, David went from college professor to unemployed husband. Gone was the cocky man who'd walked behind the lawn mower with pride. Gone was the cocky man who'd ridden his bicycle through town, head high, back straight. College professor. He'd lost his identity.

"What will we do?" Jude asked.

I imagined David teaching math at my school. The horror! I imagined him working at Dairy Queen, a white cap on his head as he passed a curled cone through the window.

"We'll have to move," he told us. "Just like everybody else. The entire faculty is leaving town. Some of them knew this was coming and already have jobs, others are looking."

"We'll never be able to sell the house," my mother said. "Not now. Think of all the homes that are going to be put on the market."

I thought about the ugly dorm buildings that littered the town. Now they would look even uglier, because they would no longer have macramé planters hanging from doorways, and bicycles chained to porch railings. They would be empty cement slabs.

"Good riddance," said old timers and not-so-old timers. "Now things will get back to the way they used to be."

We were the aliens, the foreigners, the unwelcome and uninvited.

Many of the students left town before classes ended.

"Why stay if our grades won't transfer?" they reasoned. Some remained to party until the last second. Parents and students talked of lawsuits and of trying to get at least some of their tuition back. When the day of the final class rolled around, Artesia felt like a ghost town. Maybe nobody had really thought about what a difference the loss of 10,000 people would make to a year-round population of 12,000.

David applied for teaching jobs in New Mexico, first at colleges, then high schools. Once he exhausted every available math position, he began applying anywhere and everywhere. Finally, when it seemed he would find nothing, a last-minute teaching job opened at a high school in Chicago.

I'd spent my days dreaming of the time I'd pack and leave and head back to Iowa. In my dream, David and my mother remained in New Mexico. How many times had I imagined slipping behind the wheel of some junker to get the hell out of there? The escape had been my dream, not theirs. I was supposed to be the one moving back to the Midwest.

A For Sale sign appeared in the yard, and before we left the house began to look abandoned. The lawn David had so carefully tended dried up and crunched under our feet.

"I should water it," David said.

"What difference does it make?" My mother put her hands on her hips and surveyed the dead grass. I think she was glad to be leaving, and a new place meant a new start for both of them. She was all about new starts. "Nobody will take care of it once we're gone."

We took one final drive past the college. How did desolation happen so quickly? Weeds had already sprung up in sidewalk cracks, and the swimming pool, behind a padlock, had turned a nasty shade of green. Jude and I got out of the car for a closer look and saw chairs submerged in the bottom of the pool, and beer cans floating in the gutters. I thought about the rich, suntanned girls who'd strutted around in tiny bikinis, and the draft-dodging boys who'd watched them. I remembered the excitement in David's voice as he'd told us of the plans for the college.

It all happened so fast. The beginning and the end.

This had never been my life, but I'd been drawn into it. But this was supposed to have been the beginning, the middle, and the end for David and my mother. He'd probably imagined retiring here.

"They sure do like Pabst Blue Ribbon," Jude said. We stared, fingers hooked in the chain-link fence, knuckles white.

My own identity felt different. Before, I'd been the girl who lived with the weird professor. Second-hand relevancy.

"I read that the place where we experience the most pain becomes the place that's hardest to leave," I said.

"I liked it here. So does that mean it will be easier to leave?"

"I doubt it."

My brother and I weren't close the way we used to be. He'd once been my pet, but now he was theirs. I wondered if moving would change that.

"Think we'll ever come back?" he asked.

"Probably." But I wasn't sure; Artesia was so far from the rest of the world.

We spent the next few days loading a U-Haul truck, the largest one we could get. That night we slept in sleeping bags on the floors of our empty rooms, and the next morning we rolled up the bags, brushed our teeth one last time, and took off as the sun rose, David and Jude in the truck, my mother and I following in a car packed so full we couldn't see out the back window. Twenty miles out of town, the U-Haul began to overheat. We rolled into Roswell on a choking cloud of black smoke, just making it to the place where David had rented the truck.

"Can't get a part until tomorrow," the man behind the counter said.

My mother bristled. "We have budgeted this trip down the final penny," she told him. "We can't afford an extra night on the road. I demand you pay for our motel room."

"Can't do that," the man said. "But if you want, you can sleep in the back of one of the empty trucks."

Under normal conditions she would never have accepted his offer, but I think she was tired and defeated. The truck's back door opened like a giant metal window shade, and we put our sleeping bags inside, on the wooden floor. We spent the day roaming around town, moving from shade to shade, trying to stay cool, and when the sun went down we settled into the back of the truck.

On the second day, still in New Mexico, truck repaired, we stopped to eat at a diner where the blowing sand felt like razor blades, and the sun baked our brains dry. Inside the air conditioned building, a mean waitress with a smiley-face button that said have a nice day served us hamburgers and French fries with a side order of resentment and I hate you.

The truck was still overheating. We spent hours sitting along the highway as cars roared past, waiting until dusk to travel in hopes that the engine's temperature gauge would stay out of the red. On the second night, we set up camp in the square of a little desert town in Texas.

"Is this legal?" I asked my mother.

She didn't answer.

In the middle of the night, I walked to a nearby gas station to use the restroom. The station was closed, but the Women's door was unlocked. When I stepped out, a cop was waiting for me.

"Are you with those people down there in the square?"

"Yes." I felt like some gypsy, some vagabond, and I guess I was.

"What are you doing here?"

"We're on our way to Chicago. We'll be leaving first thing in the morning."

That seemed to make him feel better. Had he thought we were going to live there?

"You can't stay the night in the square, but I'll let it go as long as you are gone tomorrow."

On the third night, I woke up to find myself alone in the car, nobody behind the wheel. It took me a moment to realize the car was attached to a wrecker, and it was being towed down the highway. I pulled my pillow against my face and went back to sleep, waking up when the truck and car finally stopped at a service station. The driver looked surprised when I crawled out of the backseat.

The next day we reached Kansas. David and my mother decided to take a shortcut to avoid rush-hour traffic. We twisted around backstreets to finally reach a bridge that was too low for the truck to pass under. We turned and retraced our path, losing hours.

When we finally made it to our new home, I was disappointed to find we wouldn't actually be living in Chicago, but rather a suburb called Western Springs. There was no time to adjust before heading to a school where cops patrolled the hallways and detectives in suits walked the perimeter. Enrollment had already taken place the previous fall, and the classes necessary for my graduation weren't available.

I was put on a Greyhound and shipped back to Artesia.

Two days later, when the bus pulled into Roswell, I spotted carloads of friends waiting for me. I stepped off the bus to laughter and hugs.

"We got you ice cream." Winona handed me a hot-fudge Sunday. "And we have a bed ready for you," she added with excitement. Arrangements had already been made; I would be living with her until graduation.

Sixteen, and my sentence was over. No more beatings, no more fear of what I would find when I stepped inside the house. The cult of two was out of my life. And when I graduated several months later at age seventeen, they didn't call and they didn't come, and I never lived with them again.

The temporary father, the pretend father, was out of my life, taking my mother with him. I'd looked forward to leaving for so long, and now I felt robbed of the statement I'd hoped to make even though the end result was the same. It was an anticlimax to years of misery. To be released with a shrug.

I didn't think it was possible for my mother to raise a child from birth to eighteen years of age, and once I was gone it was easier for her to wash her hands of the responsibility. Easier for her to forget I existed. Most of the time. She'd done so with my older brother, and now she'd let me go, and she would probably do the same with Jude.

The freedom was almost too much.

I was like some wild bird that had been kept in a cage, then finally released. I flew and flew, and beat my wings against trees and buildings and anything that got in my way. Until I received a letter from my uncle, inviting me to come and help him run his bar in Illinois.

A bar. Alcohol. I'm sure I couldn't get in any trouble there.

Chapter 25

Florida, present day

It isn't easy to find wireless internet in Ocala, Florida, but I'm sitting at a downtown café, an iced tea and blueberry scone at my elbow, laptop in front of me. I have over two hundred emails; most are newsletters and ads, maybe only twenty personal or business. It seems weeks ago that I left the Twin Cities, and weeks since I opened my laptop and communicated with the outside world, but I do a quick mental calculation and am amazed to discover it's only been a few days.

When I'm in Florida, I'm immersed in my father's world, and I bring none of my world with me. I imagine what it would be like to live here and care for him on a daily basis. I'm afraid there would be none of me left. I would be a caretaker. The person who listens to his repeated stories, the person who feeds him and makes sure he takes his medicine. I would no longer be a writer or a mother.

It's hard to go to the bathroom without an interruption, without Dad standing outside the door waiting to tell me the story he told me five minutes earlier, the same story he told me at breakfast and told me three times yesterday, so I'm surprised he didn't want to come along this morning. He got up later than usual, and I left him sitting quietly on the back porch. I suspect he took his medication twice last night, which would explain his sluggishness. Before bed, I'd checked his seven-day pill container and found today's dosage gone. Another thing to look into. A medication dispenser that worked on a timer. But I suspect the timer will only confuse him more. He needs someone to hand him the medicine and make sure he takes it.

He's been asking about my mother again, so, after replying to emails, I Google her name, not expecting to find anything. I've looked before. I'm always surprised at the number of people who don't show up in a Google search.

There's the opera star with the same name as my mother. She even lives in New Mexico, the last place it was rumored my mother was living. I try variations of names, then finally combine my mother's name with her husband's.

A funeral home website appears in the list of links.

The link takes me to my stepfather's online obituary. I check the date of death and find he's been gone a year.

As far as I know, not a single person in the family was informed of the death.

Gone.

We're included in the obituary, my brothers and I. Our names are misspelled so the obituary was most likely written by one of David's relatives, but we are there, listed as his stepchildren. The text goes into his education and where he taught, and even some things I didn't know about him. He's portrayed as a kind and gentle man who was always there to defend the weak, someone who addressed wrongs with letters to the editor of the local paper. Wrongs he could protest from a distance while my mother looked over his shoulder in approval. Maybe she'd proofed the material for him before he mailed it in, and together they were unified in their beliefs, the newspaper a way to publicly demonstrate that they were good people.

I find myself wondering if David could have been the idealized person portrayed in the obituary if he'd never met my mother. Together they'd made a toxic brew, and everybody had made excuses for David, citing his upbringing and sheltered life.

I wait to feel something, but it doesn't happen. I don't feel sad and I don't feel relieved. I feel numb. Maybe it's a conditioned response. Turning myself off was how I'd gotten through those years of living with him.

Maybe the numbness would change once the shock wore off, but I doubt it. I know I should feel something, and yet how do you mourn a man who had a negative impact on your life? I feel bad about not feeling bad.

He called me once, a couple of weeks after my mother stormed out of my hospital room. The time I almost died.

"Your mother doesn't know I'm calling," he'd said. "She doesn't want any contact with you ever again. I'm sorry. She feels betrayed because of your father. I hope you can understand."

The daring phone conversation was the first time I'd known him to go against her wishes. Poor David. My mother had been a drink of slow-acting poison he'd ingested the day they married. All he'd wanted was a family. She gave him that, but she'd also taken it away. He'd wanted to be a grandfather, and he'd given my son an antique silver cup, a cup David had used as a baby. He'd wanted his first grandchild to have it.

It was strange to follow the trail back to see how the darkness that became David's life was set in motion the day my father left my mother. It would be easy to blame Eve for everything, for the irreversible destruction to so many lives, but if it hadn't been her it would have been someone else. Some other woman would have come along and tempted my father. He was looking to sell his soul. But that theory didn't change the fact that one selfish act, the union of two selfish people, Eve and my father, had sent many lives careening out of control. Anybody along the way could have adjusted the course. My mother, my father, David, family members. My grandmother did her best, but she was afraid if she did too much my father would abandon her, too. He'd already proven he could do it. He'd already proven it was easy.

"I'll call you every month or so," David had said.

He never called back. My mother paid the bills, and he probably hadn't thought to use a payphone. She would have seen my number on the statement, and he would have been in trouble. She probably didn't speak to him for days, and I imagined him at the bedroom door, begging to be allowed in the way he'd done when we lived in Artesia.

I thought about what David's obituary would have said if his life had turned out the way he'd planned. Devoted father and grandfather, his children and grandchildren by his side when he died. He was much adored and would be greatly missed.

I don't want to feel sorry for him, and I have to remind myself of the atrocities he carried out for her. But I'd felt compassion for him even when he was beating me, and I still feel sorry for him. For his wasted life, all because he'd wanted to marry and have a family. He should never have left the Christian Brothers, poor man. Poor, poor man. Moral issues aside, he and my father were both victims of their own desires, both wanting a life they'd hoped would be more fulfilling than the one they already had. And both had allowed themselves to be bullied by women.

Of course, it's easier to have these thoughts now that David's dead. I long ago closed the door on the dark and awful years when he played the role of my father, and when I allow myself to recall those days even slightly, I feel sick to my stomach. But blaming him is like blaming a gun for killing someone.

No, that's not the right way to think about it. He was human. He made choices. Terrible choices. We are all in control of our lives.

I want to tell the parents of the world to teach their children to think for themselves. To question authority. To question everything. I've seen and experienced the product of blind faith. They were a cult of two, and my mother was David's charismatic leader.

"I took a vow to her, not you," David told Jude when my brother asked his stepfather to stand up for him years later. The man I'd thought would vanish from our lives in a year or two had remained by my mother's side for thirty years.

I've taken a vow.

Had he ever regretted marrying her? Or had he not allowed his thoughts to even go there?

I'd known David less than three years, and I'd never accepted him as my father or stepfather, but he'd been the only father Jude had known. It was hard to keep track of who was in and out of my mother's favor, but since the news of David's death hadn't hit the circle of relatives, I guessed she wasn't in touch with anyone. I email the link to both of my brothers and several other relatives. Would the relatives even want to know? Would they even care? Or would the news be traumatic for them, not because of the death, but because it would bring back memories better left forgotten?

It's a fairly long obituary, and I read it several times. One line keeps jumping out at me: *Survived by his wife.*

She was still alive. Or was she? If she died, who would post an online obituary? How would any of her relatives know?

The text said David had lived in Albuquerque, so I do a little more searching using that location. A newspaper article pops up. It's an interview with a retired woman who is complaining about the increase in rent in her low-income apartment. The woman is my mother, and the article includes a photo.

Of an old woman with gray hair, sitting in a living room reading a self-help book. I check the date of the article and find it was written two months ago. It gives the name of the apartment complex, and the Albuquerque suburb. She always insisted upon an unlisted number, but with a little more searching I find a political campaign website that lists the addresses and phone numbers of contributors. My mother's address and phone number is there.

I pull a tablet from my bag and jot down the information while bookmarking the pages. As an added precaution, I do a screen capture of everything.

By the time I'm done, both of my brothers have emailed back. They are stunned, but my younger brother is understandably the most upset. Angry that our mother couldn't have made the effort to let him know. David would have wanted us to know.

I close the laptop and head back to Dad's. I hope he hasn't been waiting for me to return. Sometimes he gets annoyed and irritated to be kept waiting, and other times he doesn't seem to notice that the day has passed. Today is like that. He seemed unruffled as I step inside, almost as if he hadn't noticed I was gone. Or, more likely, he'd forgotten I was visiting.

He does this thing where he braces himself, legs apart, and leans forward, arms hanging at his sides. "What about lunch?" he says, making the kind of face you might use when playing with a dog, talking in a teasing, jovial voice.

I look at the clock on the wall. It's almost 1:00.

He can mix himself a drink, but I've never seen him get anything to eat. On weekends, Carol leaves prepared food in the refrigerator in clear containers so he will see it. When he gets hungry enough, he sometimes opens the containers, but more often he goes to the bar.

"Where did you go?" he asks as we sit down to leftovers I made of the chicken tacos.

"To a café so I could check my email." I know he won't be able to grasp what I'm talking about. Email is a hard concept for him, and a café is harder, and the Internet impossible. Mail comes in the mailbox at the end of the driveway.

But he's good at playing along. "Did you have any?"

"Quite a few that I had to answer."

"What kind of work do you do?" He understands that the email might have to do with a job.

"I'm a writer."

Dad could talk and talk about the past, and relate events coherently, but he has a hard time processing what other people say. I keep my sentences short and simple, and avoid speaking more than a few of them at a time.

He tries to hide his confusion.

"I write books." Referring to a physical object helps him understand.

"Oh. That's right." His face clears.

I think about the address and the phone number in my bag. I can almost feel it in there, and I almost expect it to start glowing.

She's alive.

Dad's alive.

Eve is dead.

David is dead.

If this were a romance, the obvious thing would be to get my parents back together. And even though I'm an adult with kids of my own, maybe I still want that, still fantasize about something ridiculous. Dad thinks he's young and hot; I doubt he'll want anything to do with the old lady in the news article. I once took him to a senior citizen's bingo event, and he'd looked around with disgust, proclaiming everybody there to be *old*. One woman who was quite a bit younger stopped to welcome him. He got her phone number and began calling her as soon as we returned home. He didn't stop until she told him she was happily married.

I wonder if my mother still has the wedding gown and the wedding album. I imagine both are the color of coffee stains. I wonder if David has faded in the way Eve has faded for my father, replaced by stronger memories of the past.

Silly thoughts. I'm creating a plot in my head. In real life, they would meet and my father would wonder who the old lady was, and the old lady would pick up a knife and stab him in the chest for leaving her all those years ago. No, she would just stare at him with cold, cold eyes. And then she would tell him she hoped he rotted in hell and it served him right that he had dementia, although now he can no longer remember the awful things he's done to people. She would leave, and, two minutes after she left, Dad would say, "What do you hear from your mother?"

And then my mother would go home and write a long, nasty letter that would arrive in the mailbox at the end of the driveway. When he opened the letter, he would pore over the words without grasping the meaning of them. And when he was done, he would fold the letter and think about giving her a call.

People with Alzheimer's still feel emotion, but they lack the ability to control that emotion because they can't recall the source, can't recall the trigger. But the emotion, whether happy or sad, lingers. Like waking up from a dream you can't recall, yet carrying the sorrow of that dream with you throughout the day.

My visits make my dad sad and he doesn't know why. My presence takes his thoughts in a direction he can no longer control, and I wonder if he would be better off if I never came to see him at all. For both of us, it's a house of horrors where every time we turn some unpleasant memory pops up.

"Do you remember me and Thomas as children?" I ask as I wash the dishes and Dad sits at the table. Occasionally, I start the trips down memory lane. "When we lived in Miami Beach?"

"No. Who did you live with?"

"You."

"Me? Why would you live with me?"

"You're my father."

"I am?" And then he gets flustered. "Of course I am."

I was so young, and my own recall is more an emotional recall than an actual ability to replay events. It's the excitement I would feel when he came home in the evening. I felt loved, and I now wonder if that emotion was real, or if he just smiled at me the way he smiles at everybody.

He never spanked me, never yelled at me, never raised his voice. Maybe that's what I responded to.

And if he'd loved me at one time … it made his abandonment all the more puzzling. It made it worse.

He'd been seduced. Not by a beautiful woman, but a lifestyle. He'd left us for a lifestyle.

Alzheimer's isn't just about forgetting. Alzheimer's sometimes rewrites the past, and the stories Dad recounts in such detail aren't always true. I sometimes wonder if his memories become the way he wishes things had been.

I've done my homework, and I know Alzheimer's is hereditary. Every time I forget something, I wonder if this is it. Not those misplacing-my-keys moments, but watching a movie and wondering if I've watched it before. Forgetting where I spent last Christmas, and losing track of how long I've lived where I now live. How many seasons have gone by. Those moments when I feel blank, hollow. Being unable to put a name to a face, and unable to recall streets. The fear of it happening to me is with me every day.

How many years before he reached this point? Ten? Maybe fifteen when he started showing early signs of dementia. About the time my husband died. Dad came to the funeral, and I chalked up his odd behavior to the situation. We were all under stress. If it happens, if I lose touch, I know I might not have the capacity to realize it. I might not be able to tell my children not to spend the best years of their lives taking care of me.

I don't want to be a potato with a heartbeat.

How perfectly annoying it will be if the one thing my father gives me is Alzheimer's.

"If you had Nan's address, would you write to her?" I ask. "If you had her number, would you call her?"

"Oh, I don't know."

I dig the address and phone number from my bag. I won't call for him. I won't write for him. I'll give him the address and phone number and let him decide.

"What's this?" he asked, holding the paper in both hands.

I tell him. "In case you ever want it."

Without hesitation, he picks up the phone and dials the number.

Chapter 26

The phone calls to Nan go unanswered, and I'm not sure how many voicemails Dad leaves over the course of the afternoon. And because he doesn't remember that he's already called her, he tries again. I regret giving him the number, and I wonder how long it will be before he forgets he has it. Soon, I hope.

I imagine my mother in her New Mexico apartment, seeing his name on her Caller ID. Staring at it in horror, wondering, What in the hell ...? I shouldn't have given him the number. But if I hadn't ... I didn't want to regret not doing it.

Eventually, the boredom of the day settles around us. I pace the living room, looking at the framed photos of Eve scattered throughout the house. I finally come across one of my dad. He's standing in profile, knees slightly bent, embracing a Dalmatian.

The dog is on its back legs, paws wrapped around my father. My gaze shifts to the background and I notice an airstrip with a private plane. I'm guessing the plane is Dad's. The colors in the photo are faded, with a yellow cast to everything.

"What dog is this?" I ask, pointing.

Dad shuffles up beside me, neck craned, mouth open slightly as he gauges the photo. I can feel him connect and fall into the past. His shoulders relax and his eyes light up. "That's Archie," he tells me. "Do you know the story of Archie?"

"No."

"Eve bought him as a show dog, but it turned out he wasn't what the owner claimed he was. So when I was at work she shipped him back." He points at the photo. "I flew across the country to get him. That picture was taken right after I landed."

A beautiful story, yes. On the surface. He'd flown across the country to reunite with a dog. He'd gone out of his way for an animal he adored.

I continue staring at the photo while Dad vanishes down the hall. I hear drawers opening and closing, and then he reappears, a fat manila envelope in his hand. He places it on the table, then steps back like a proud child. He wants me to open it; he wants me to look inside.

I pull out a chair and sit down. I open the thick envelope and realize it consists of what looks like everything my brothers and I have ever sent him over the span of our lives. Letters, newspaper articles, photos. Sad, pathetic pleas for his attention, for just a small acknowledgment, a response.

I find a newspaper interview of my older brother. He'd won a prestigious photography award. In the margins of the clipping is handwriting elaborating on the interview, explaining how the reporter got a few things wrong, and the notes are my brother's revisions to make clear what had really taken place. The notes themselves feel personal, meant for Dad's eyes only, a son begging his father to take notice. I've done the same.

I fold the article and put it down. We all did it, my brothers and I. Even after we became adults we wanted him to notice us. Maybe this would be a big enough accomplishment to get his attention. Maybe this time he would call or let me know he'd received my letter.

He never responded, yet he'd kept everything.

Why was he showing me this? Was he proud that he'd made the connection between the letters in the drawer and me? Or was he subconsciously saying, *See, I didn't forget you completely. I kept these things. I kept the letters and the photos and the newspaper clippings. And because I kept them, I wasn't the bad father you thought I was.*

The letter I mailed to him from Artesia is there, the letter with the drawing of the shell, the letter I wrote after I broke a sweet boy's fragile heart. I can't bear to read it, so I set it aside and pick up a snapshot of a girl in a Catholic-school uniform. I remember it; remember the day, the photo taken shortly after we moved back to Iowa. I would have been about eight. My hair is in braids, and I have dark circles under my eyes. I look sick and malnourished. It would have been taken during the time my older brother and I went to school hungry, the time I often struggled to stay awake at night to care for my baby brother while I imagined my father with a drink in one hand, a cigarette in the other, his head tipped back in laughter.

"Who's that?" my father asks.

"Me." Every day that I'm here, my life flashes before my eyes. Things I don't want to think about, things I don't want to remember.

A month ago, he would have known everything about it. This is the change I've noticed this trip. The memories of the past that have been vivid and perfect, are now eroding, being eaten away. I imagine moth-eaten fabric full of black holes that will continue to grow larger until there is nothing left but dust.

I shuffle through the photos. I don't want to look, but I can't help myself. The wound has already been reopened.

Pictures of me and my older brother, standing on the front step of our grandmother's house. Our faces are incredibly sober, like a couple of pioneers, and we are just an hour away from walking into a new school. My brother has dark curly hair that looks exactly like Dad's looked before it went white. On the back of the photo, in my grandmother's handwriting, are names and dates.

Dad is looking at the newspaper article about Thomas and his photography. I wonder what he's thinking until he turns the paper around so I can see it more clearly. "Who's this?"

"Thomas."

"Who's Thomas?"

"Your son."

He knows, and yet he doesn't know. On some level, he's made the connection. Otherwise, why had he dug out the photos and presented them to me? But on another level, he doesn't recognize these people. On another level, he's trying to figure out who I am, and what I'm doing in his house. When you think about Alzheimer's, you think about memory loss, but you don't think about the mental confusion.

Now he's holding the photo of me.

"That was taken when I lived in Burlington, Iowa, right after you and Mom divorced," I tell him.

"Burlington …" He gives that some thought. "It was a shame when they tore down all of those old homes to put in the freeway." Inside his brain, things are falling into place. I sometimes imagine his mind as a bunch of wires with sparks flying from the ends. The wind blows and the wires touch, connect, and for a few moments he suddenly knows who I am, and maybe he even knows he's sitting in his own house.

"Your mom had a maternity shop, didn't she?"

"Yes."

"Where was that located?" He pauses, thinking. "North Hill, wasn't it? Where all the old Victorian houses were."

"Yes."

We pack up the articles and the photos and put them back in the envelope, then we head down the hall.

"A stork on the building," he says, opening the bedroom door.

I nod, remembering it too. I'd forgotten about the stork. Painted on one entire side of the brick building.

"Holding a white bundle in its beak," I say.

The drawer beside the bed is open, almost falling out. Dad places the packet inside and I now realize that these things are kept beside his bed, just a foot from the pillow where he sleeps.

"With a baby." He's accessed his past, and his memory is suddenly better than mine. The past isn't made up of dangling wires that blow in the wind. The past is either here or not, and always more real and more alive than the present. He wanders around inside his brain, where those things are stored, and when he finds something of interest, he opens a drawer and pulls it out, and it's as fresh and as real as the day he put it away. As if it's been waiting for him all of this time, for just this moment, a room filled from ceiling to floor with rich stories that he can smell and touch and recall as if the event took place moments ago, easier to recall than today's visit to the doctor or the conversation we just had about my Catholic school photo. Recent memories don't get vaulted, don't get stored and caressed and saved. And maybe they don't deserve to be saved. Maybe they don't matter. Because for him, the richness of life is gone. There are just the days of feeding the dogs and going to the bar, and dreaming of conversations with a young waitress.

He shuts the drawer, and we move out of the room and down the carpeted hall.

Maybe that girl in the manila envelope reminds him of another life, another time, when he was young and strong and handsome, a time when woman fought over him, when women cried over him, when women didn't forget him. When he impacted and damaged lives in his young ignorance, in his hot-headed passion for living that left us all behind because we were encumbered, we were held down by responsibility and doing what was right, while he simply went after whatever he wanted, who he wanted, with no thought of the trail of chaos he left behind. Those were the things he embraced then, and they are the things he embraces now. Those vivid memories take him away from the drudgery he spent his entire life avoiding, the drudgery of this room and this chair and these walls and the low ceiling that presses down on us, the windows that are smeared from dog noses that constantly watch for something that will never come. And back in the bedroom, next to the bed, the drawer is overflowing with the photos and letters that meant nothing to him when his life was full, just a curiosity and a guilt, something he didn't want to look at, didn't want to think about, but couldn't bring himself to throw away.

Now those pictures reside there, calling to him throughout the remainder of his days. He gets them out, he stares at them, and, in the quiet tedium, he wonders who these people are, and wonders what they once meant to him. The answer fails to come, but an emotion he doesn't understand remains, an artifact, and he finds himself going back so that he can feel it again. He spreads the photos on his bed, and he reads the articles, and the guilt rises up, and also a compelling connection to the girl in the Catholic jumper, and the smiling boy with the dark curls. He feels compelled to look, to experience, to embrace that emotion. And once he is full, he gets up, he goes to the living room, and he sits down.

The mood of the mysterious children, the feeling their images brought to his day, lingers. Occasionally he thinks about them, and he might even find himself going back to the bedroom, opening the drawer, and pulling out the photos to once again spread them on the bed, forgetting that he'd done it just hours ago.

He will look at them. He will embrace the emotion, and later he will sit in a chair in front of the window and wait for the mysterious children to come home.

Chapter 27

I'm struck by the similarities between today and the Florida of my childhood.   A father. A daughter. Sunlight and palm trees. A car that will take me to the airport, a plane that will carry me high in the air while my father remains on the ground. In my mind, I see him shrink until he vanishes and clouds cover the spot where he stands. All these years later, he has returned to the scene of the crime.

I recall the words he spoke to me so long ago. "You will never see or hear from me again. Don't look for me, don't wait for me, I won't be coming. I won't be back."

He wasn't going off to war, he wasn't going to prison, he hadn't volunteered for a combat mission that would end in certain death, he wasn't dying of cancer. He just wanted a new life. My brothers and I were the ratty clothes he'd peeled off, shoved into a plastic bag, and tossed in the garbage. We were the cement blocks cut from his ankles as he kicked his way to the surface. We were his buzz kill.

He follows me to the rental car. We hug. He kisses my cheek, and for a moment I can almost smell salt-water, the varnish of a boat deck, and the aftershave he hasn't used in years. I open the door, get behind the wheel, and lower the window so we can talk.

Alzheimer's has removed the chance of my being able to find closure and possibly forgive him. I always thought someday we would discuss what happened, and maybe I would eventually come to understand why he did what he did. But now, even when he's right in front of me, I know I'll never have the answers I need. Everything is unfinished.

The past calls to me too, and I find myself wondering about the desert town where I spent my teenage years. In my mind, I return to New Mexico and visit the place where I cared for Estelle, the town where my mother lived with David, the stranger who changed our lives in the most awful of ways.

In my mind, our old house is tiny. Almost like a toy.

It seems melodramatic to say that my mother and her husband robbed me and my brother of our childhood, but it's true. We had beds, we had food. They didn't lock us in closets. They didn't make us fashion lampshades from our own skin. But when I imagine the house I shared with them, I feel sick.

As I stand in the street, I see my little brother dressed in my mother's wedding gown, the gown she wore the day she married my father. Jude is moving back and forth in front of the window, and my mother is laughing. Outside, David pushes a lawnmower across the yard, his back and arms stiff with pride, his head high, a married man. I'm inside, behind the white curtains with lavender tassels, waiting for it all to end.

And I can't help but know deep in my heart that my father is responsible for this dark chapter of our lives. And I will never have closure, because he will never have the chance to justify his actions, or help me to understand, at least a little.

Forty years ago, I cared for Estelle. And in forty years, nothing has changed other than medication that can sometimes control the symptoms of Alzheimer's for a period of time. No advances have been made as far as a cure. My father's own doctor shrugs and says

Alzheimer's is simply an unfortunate part of aging. He's wrong. It's a disease in need of a cure.

The elderly flock to Florida where care is limited. The state medical system can't handle them all, and Alzheimer's patients like my father go without the care and therapy they need. And people might say, 'Oh, this is Florida. That's why. Simply too many elderly in Florida.' But Florida is the canary. Twenty million Alzheimer's patients are coming, and they will spread across the country.

"I wish you could stay longer," Dad says. "I hope you can come back soon."

He never reached my mother. All for the best. An unknown woman who identified herself as my mother's sister-in-law finally called back and told him to quit bothering them. She said Nan was out of the country.

In the past, when I've left, my father has cried, but this time there are no tears. His mind has moved to another stage of Alzheimer's, and I wonder if he's thinking about going to Home Plate; I wonder if he's thinking about Octavia.

"I'll be back in a few months," I tell him.

"That would be great." But he doesn't seem connected to the conversation, almost as if he's looking forward to my leaving. I've upset the pattern of his days.

Next time he won't know me. He won't recognize me at all. What little memory he has of us together will be gone for good.

The tables have turned and I'm the one trying to hold back tears thinking of the father who took me high in the crow's nest, thinking the years that have passed and the things that will never be.

I start the rental car and put it in gear. I wave, and he waves back. I pull away and look at him in the rearview mirror. And I know he's erasing me one last time.

Author's note: Timelines in The Man Who Left were condensed for the sake of pacing. Names were changed to protect the privacy of individuals, and some people are composites.

About the Author

Theresa Weir (a.k.a. Anne Frasier) is a *New York Times* and *USA Today* bestselling author of twenty-five books and numerous short stories that have spanned the genres of suspense, mystery, thriller, romantic suspense, paranormal, fantasy, and memoir. During her award-winning career, she's written for Penguin Putnam, Simon & Schuster, HarperCollins Publishers, Bantam Books/Random House, Silhouette Books, Grand Central Publishing/Hachette, and Thomas & Mercer. Her titles have been printed in both hardcover and paperback and translated into twenty languages.

Her first memoir, THE ORCHARD, was a 2011 Oprah Magazine Fall Pick, Number Two on the Indie Next list, a featured B+ review in Entertainment Weekly, and a Librarians' Best Books of 2011. Her second memoir, THE MAN WHO LEFT, was a *New York Times* Bestseller. Going back to 1988, Weir's debut title was the cult phenomenon AMAZON LILY, initially published by Pocket Books and later reissued by Bantam Books. Writing as Theresa Weir, she won a RITA for romantic suspense (COOL SHADE), and a year later the Daphne du Maurier for paranormal romance (BAD KARMA). In her more recent Anne Frasier career, her thriller and suspense titles hit the *USA Today* list (HUSH, SLEEP TIGHT, PLAY DEAD) and were featured in Mystery Guild, Literary Guild, and Book of the Month Club. HUSH was both a RITA and Daphne du Maurier finalist. Well-known in the mystery community, she served as hardcover judge for the Thriller presented by International Thriller Writers, and was guest of honor at the Diversicon 16 mystery/science fiction conference held in Minneapolis in 2008. Frasier books have received high praise from print publications such as *Publishers Weekly, Minneapolis Star Tribune,* and *Crimespree,* as well as online praise from *Spinetingler, Book Loons, Armchair Interviews, Sarah Weinman's Confessions of an Idiosyncratic Mind,* and Ali Karim's *Shots Magazine.* Her books have featured cover quotes from Lisa Gardner, Jane Ann Krentz, Linda Howard, Kay Hooper, J.A. Konrath, Jamie Ford, and Nicholas Sparks. She is a member of Sisters in Crime and International Thriller Writers.

www.theresaweir.com

BP
Belfry Press

CPSIA information can be obtained at www.ICGtesting.com
Printed in the USA
LVOW11s1909240315

431820LV00005B/618/P